Merry Christmas
To Roy and Esther
With love from
Rodger and Trudy

PHILIP MELANCHTHON
Reformer Without Honor

by

MICHAEL ROGNESS

Augsburg Publishing House
Minneapolis   Minnesota

PHILIP MELANCHTHON

Manufactured in the United States of America

To Eva

with gratitude
for those good years
when this was written

Foreword

History has granted Philip Melanchthon a strange place. He was Luther's most important co-worker, yet he is quite unknown outside theological circles. Luther considered him an invaluable spokesman and diplomat, yet many today insist that he betrayed and misrepresented Luther. Conservative Lutherans bitterly criticize him, yet they themselves are often strongly "Melanchthonian" in their concern for "pure doctrine" and in their views on the key doctrine of justification.

Melanchthon's works are not widely known; indeed, they are seldom read. We have learned of him largely through second-hand opinions, and he had the unhappy experience of being caricatured by friends and foes alike. One of the side effects of the burst of research on Luther in this century is that Melanchthon finally is finding his own proper place beside Luther.

The two men were different. Many deplore this fact, but in terms of Reformation history this was a fortunate circumstance. Where one man was weak, the other was strong. On countless occasions, where one lacked the temperament to do well, the other stepped in and represented the Reformation with great ability.

The confessional hostility of past centuries is finally giving way to the conviction that believers from each Christian tradition are brothers. But, ironically, an "ecumenicist" must be a "confessionalist" as well. Ecumenical dialogue requires openness and is fruitful only when the participants can speak of their own tradition with knowledge and competence. The broad question behind this volume is: What *is* "Lutheran" theology? The specific purpose of the book is to define Melanchthon's place in the development of this theology.

First, we shall watch a theology being born and molded in its early years. "Lutheran theology" is for us today a rather complete set of convictions, handed down through four centuries. It is difficult to realize that it was quite a different story in the first years of the Reformation. Luther began it, not with a theology but with what he believed to be a rediscovery of basic Gospel truths concerning God's grace. Out of this rediscovery came a theology, a thorough reflection to support these convictions and sound reasoning to draw out the vast implications of Reformation principles. Church history furnished many possible patterns. Many topics could be colored by this or that nuance, borrowing from one or another pre-Reformation school of thought. It was a time when the evangelicals were feeling their way toward a full theology.

Melanchthon came to the Reformation as a Humanist. For him the first years in Wittenberg were a time of sifting, sorting, and considering various kinds of theological expressions. Regular contact, discussion, and deepening friendship with Luther had a profound impact on the young teacher. Finally his thoughts began to crystallize, and from his early works we see his mature theology emerging. We shall try to trace this process and pinpoint the causes behind this development.

Second, we shall outline this mature theology. To understand Lutheran theology at all, one must deal with Melanchthon. It was he, more than Luther, who was the classroom teacher of succeeding Lutheran theologians. Ernst Troeltsch wrote toward the end of the last century:

> It was not Luther but Melanchthon who determined fully what the exact consistency of Lutheranism was to be. He was the chief teacher and instructor, the scholarly publicist, and the theological diplomat of early Lutheranism; as such he passed Luther's ideas through the sieve of his formulations. (Quoted from Prof. Wilhelm Pauck's lecture, "Luther and Melanchthon.")

We shall not only examine the formation of Melanchthon's theology but observe the threads which are drawn from there into the Formula of Concord and the later age of orthodoxy. Since much of the misunderstanding surrounding Melanchthon stems from the controversies of his old age, the last chapter deals with them briefly but specifically. Throughout the book we shall refer to Luther's own thought, although an adequate comparison of the two men would require a large volume of its own.

It is obvious that a book of this size must do a great deal of summarizing. It is also clear that some areas of Melanchthon's thought will scarcely be touched upon. The book will deal with the heart of his theology—sin, law, gospel, Christ, justification, new life—the historically crucial themes of his thought.

This book grew out of a doctoral dissertation. Gratitude is due to many people, but particularly to Prof. Wilhelm Maurer of Erlangen University, who was to me a *Doktorvater* in the very real sense of the word. There may be readers who wish to refer to the original thesis, but they should be forewarned that it is in German, rather lengthy and loaded with footnotes. Hopefully, this condensed version will contribute to a more accurate understanding of the "teacher of the Reformation."

MICHAEL ROGNESS

Centre d'Etudes Oecuméniques
Strasbourg, France

Contents

CHAPTER ONE

Reformer

In the late summer of 1518 the new professor of Greek rode into the university town of Wittenberg. Philip Melanchthon was only 21 years old but had already attracted attention as one of the young prodigies in German academic circles. He was accustomed to the exciting atmosphere of the great universities of Heidelberg and Tübingen, where he had earned his bachelor of arts and master of arts degrees. Wittenberg must have seemed dull at first glance—a provincial, out-of-the-way school in a small town, with no traditions stretching into past centuries.

Little did the young teacher know that he was to be plunged into a lifetime of exhausting activity, for even then Wittenberg was about to become the storm center of the greatest upheaval Europe had known in centuries. One of Melanchthon's colleagues was an outspoken Saxon monk, Martin Luther. Only months before, Luther had posted on the door of the castle church a list of 95 statements concerning the common practice of indulgences. This initial protest gave birth to the Reformation, and this movement found its spokesman in the articulate Melanchthon.

1

In August 1518, however, the young professor was unaware of these rumblings. He was neither a clergyman nor a theologian; he was a classical Humanist. To understand Melanchthon we must begin by understanding the Humanism of the day.

Humanism

The impetus behind Humanism was the Renaissance rediscovery of man. The Humanists sought to escape the harsh life and somber tones of the Dark Ages and recapture the grandeur of ancient Greece and Rome. They gloried in the beauty of nature and the capacity of man's spirit. In contrast to the weighty Latin theological tomes of the preceding centuries, secular literature written in the vernacular began to bloom. Dante's *Divine Comedy* combined religious fervor with the secular figures of Virgil and Beatrice. Petrarch with his lyrics of love and Boccaccio with his bawdy *Decameron* delighted the senses of liberated readers. Man's creativity was given free reign in painting, sculpture, architecture, music, and all culture.

The church was not unaffected. The awe and respect the educated held for the church was tarnished when the shrewd Lorenzo Valla, armed with Humanist scholarship, proved the Donation of Constantine* a forgery, undermining papal claims of temporal power. He also demonstrated linguistic flaws in the Latin Vulgate version of the Bible. The papal

---

*The Donation of Constantine was a document fabricated during the eighth or ninth century A.D. which purportedly came from Emperor Constantine and conferred upon the pope dominion over all Italy and other areas "of the Western regions."

court succumbed to the spirit of Humanism by imitating fancy court style, launching magnificent building projects and tolerating a mixture of pagan and Christian motifs in its works of art.

The goal of a Humanist was to become a highly educated and cultured person. The universities and academies were his laboratories, and almost all the outstanding Humanists were equally famous as teachers. At the universities the Humanists looked to the enlightened men of Greece and Rome for their ideals and steeped themselves in the philosophy, literature, and culture of that era. *"Ad fontes"* was their battle-cry—"Back to the sources!" To recapture this bygone age, a primary task was to learn its languages: Plato's Greek and Cicero's Latin. John Reuchlin, one of south Germany's greatest Humanists, also spearheaded the resurgence of Hebrew studies. Reuchlin was Melanchthon's great-uncle and had carefully supervised the linguistic training of his talented nephew.

But there was a great difference between the Humanism of the Italian Renaissance and that of northern Europe. Southern European Humanism was sophisticated and secular. The Humanism north of the Alps was deeply colored by the piety and mysticism of the late Middle Ages. With its beginnings among such mystics as Meister Eckhart and the "Friends of God," this *devotio moderna* (literally "new devotion") found its strongest influence in the "Brethren of the Common Life." Founded more than a century before the Reformation, this group flourished in Holland and northern Germany. Through its schools it molded the faith of hundreds of young scholars.

The *devotio moderna* was, above all, a return to the Christ-centered life of Christian love. It was not interested in the imposing edifice of Scholastic dogma, but emphasized an internal and personal union with Christ. It was this piety which gave us one of the jewels among devotional works, Thomas à Kempis' *Imitation of Christ,* the classic statement of the *devotio moderna.*

Northern European Humanism was best characterized by its most illustrious exponent, Erasmus of Rotterdam. Erasmus was brought up in the Brethren's schools of Deventer and Bois le Duc. He became a cosmopolitan scholar, well-traveled in Humanist circles and acquainted with all the glittering names among the Humanists. Though his acid comments on the church of his day (*Praise of Folly,* for example) appealed to the more cynical, secular Humanists, they came from a heart imbued with this new piety. Erasmus was the idol of all young German scholars, including the youthful Melanchthon.

Although Erasmus never joined the Reformers and broke sharply and bitterly with Luther, he still must be reckoned as a figure on the threshold of the Reformation.[1] His criticisms of the Roman Catholic hierarchy were as caustic as any made by Luther. His edition of the Greek New Testament became a Reformation (and Luther's) textbook. His studies of the church fathers opened new horizons in understanding the ancient church, and one cannot miss the evangelical note all through his New Testament commentaries, the *Paraphrases.*

Though deeply disappointed by the rupture between Erasmus and Luther, Melanchthon managed to maintain cordial relations with the great Humanist.[2] Indeed, Melanchthon's desire to maintain contact with his many Humanist friends often was cited by his critics as a sign of vacillating allegiance to the Reformation.

Humanism and Scholasticism

It is no wonder that the Humanists had so little interest in scholasticism. On almost every issue they were at opposite poles. For example:

1. The Scholastics concentrated on doctrine; the Humanists were interested in practical, ethical living. A Scholastic theologian mistrusted the Humanist because of his disregard for orthodox dogma. A Humanist scoffed at scholasticism as so much time wasted on futile speculation. Melanchthon insisted that "no faithful man has ever satisfied his mind with Scholastic theology which has become polluted by so many human arguments, nonsense, tricks, and trifling traditions." [3]

2. The schoolmen were both theologians and philosophers. They used the language of philosophy liberally. The Humanists also considered themselves philosophers, but disliked the intricacies of Scholastic philosophy. They advocated what they termed the "philosophy of Christ," a mixture of biblical teachings and ethics with a Platonic tint inherited from the Neo-platonism of the Italian Humanists.[4] This was not speculative but practical, they insisted; the "philosophy of Christ" freed them from the clutches of their baser passions into true life. This ethical

interest in philosophy and doctrine was reflected by the young Melanchthon.

3. Even when the Scholastics considered practical living, they did so on a different plane than the Humanists. The schoolmen looked to the accumulated traditions of monastic morality and its merits. The Humanist shrugged this off as irrelevant and turned instead to the simple advice and example of Jesus himself.

4. Each side had sharply different views of church history. The Scholastics looked upon their age as the summit of the development of Christian thought. The Humanists went back to the sources for their standards. Their goal of Christlike, spiritual living they found, above all, in the Bible. Next to the Bible, they esteemed the church fathers. For a Humanist, Scholasticism had strayed too far from the sources. It is no wonder that the Reformation *sola scriptura* principle found hearty applause among the Humanists.[5]

5. Faith itself was conceived in diverging fashions. For the Scholastics, faith was intimately connected with the sacramental structure of the church. One must cling to the system of grace imparted in the sacraments. The Humanists disliked not only the bureaucracy of the church, but its ceremony as well. Nourished in mysticism, they shunned the outward trappings and looked inwardly to a union with Christ. Here again, the Reformation found enthusiastic support from the Humanists. This contempt for the sacramental system as the sole dispenser of

grace brought Erasmus under ominous suspicion from the ecclesiastical inquisitors.

Melanchthon's Opening Lecture

One week after his arrival in Wittenberg, Melanchthon presented his introductory lecture, "On Improving the Studies of Youth." His proposals for revising the university curriculum and his goals for education drew strong approval from Luther, who was present to hear the young professor.[6]

Melanchthon criticized the late Middle Ages' practice of relying on commentaries and secondary sources. He advocated a firm foundation in Latin, Greek, and Hebrew, so that students could study the sources themselves. The life of a Christian would thus be renewed, for he would be drawing directly from the biblical teachings of Christ. Melanchthon also outlined plans to broaden training in history, mathematics, and science.

The lecture was a resounding success. Melanchthon had combined the goals of the Humanists with the concerns of Luther's young reform movement. Even though Melanchthon was not to cast his lot publicly with Luther and the Reformation until almost a year later at the Leipzig debate, Luther already recognized his young colleague as a providential addition to the Wittenberg faculty.

The LOCI COMMUNES—the "Benefits of Christ"

The work that won for Melanchthon the reputation as "teacher" of the Reformation was his *Loci Communes* of 1521.[7] In the opening paragraphs he used the phrase which

became his best-known and most characteristic statement:
"To know Christ is to know his benefits."

This opening manifesto was the cry of both the Humanist
and the Reformer who said the monumental topics of the
Scholastics—God, God's unity and trinity, creation, the mode
of the incarnation—were not matters for endless speculation,
but should be accepted in faith. The Scholastic theologians,
Melanchthon claimed, had become "vain in their discussions,
while wasting a whole lifetime over universals, formalities,
connotations, and I know not what other meaningless
words." [8]

The real issues, Melanchthon continued, were not these
great mysteries, but the practical concerns of sin, law, and
grace. Through them we learn of Christ's *beneficia,* his
saving work of redemption. We come to know Christ when
we know him as Savior. [9]

The theme "to know Christ is to know his benefits" was
heartily endorsed by Luther. Christ's benefits, his saving
mission, were, after all, the heart of the Reformation message. [10] This emphasis was met with equal approval from the
Humanists. Indeed, Melanchthon found the term "benefits of
Christ" or "benefits of God" in Erasmus' *Paraphrasis* of
Romans and his *Ratio seu Methodus.* For Erasmus the
beneficium dei meant God's graciousness of benevolence in
a general sense, but it also referred specifically to Christ's
saving work. [11]

This phrase, therefore, gives us one example of how Melanchthon used his Humanist background as a Reformer. He
narrowed down Erasmus' general meaning to the specific

beneficia of Christ.[12] The word *beneficium-beneficia* is understood in its literal Latin sense as "good act" or "salutary deed," referring directly to the saving work of Christ, the center of Reformation theology.

So the opening paragraphs of the first Reformation textbook combine Melanchthon's Humanist background with the Reformation message. Doctrinal speculation and theological systems give way to the towering biblical themes of law, sin, and grace—not abstract matters, but the living concerns of each believer. The Gospel is centered in the benefits of Christ, a term taken from Humanism and fitted into the new evangelical proclamation.

Man's Sin

One of the sharpest differences between the Humanists and the Reformation grew out of their basically contradictory views of man. The clash between these two outlooks is one of the dominant features in Melanchthon's early works.

In its concept of man, Humanism assumed a dualism of body and reason, of fleshly and spiritual natures. This, of course, is not surprising, considering its background of mysticism and Neoplatonism. The clearest example of this dualism in north European Humanism can be found in Erasmus' best-seller, the *Enchiridion of a Christian Soldier,* a practical handbook for living a Christian life.

The result of the Humanist's dualism was that he saw sin located primarily in the flesh or body. Man's reason, spirit, or soul was inherently noble, he reasoned. It might be mired down by the sins of the flesh, but it was not the seat of sin, and it reached upward to escape the clutches of lust. This viewpoint had two significant implications:

1. A Humanist did not take sin as seriously as did a Reformer. After all, the Humanist said, since only the lower nature of man was innately sinful, man's reason or spirit could struggle to lift itself up. Luther's spiritual torments, where he saw the deep impurity most of all in his reason and spirit, were utterly unknown and incomprehensible to the Humanist.

2. Since sin was the oppression of man's flesh over his reason and spirit, the redemptive work of Christ must be to free man's higher nature from its bondage to his lower nature so that the spirit of man could soar in enlightened harmony with God's spirit.

In his first years at Wittenberg, Melanchthon often used dualist language. Many of his sentences could as easily have been written by Erasmus. For example, in his Humanist-colored lectures on the Gospel of Matthew in 1519-1520 he wrote, "Indeed, one will never become perfect until our flesh is first reduced to ashes." [13] In his lecture on "Paul and the Scholastics" he expressed himself again in Humanist terms: "A manifold cupidity exercises its tyranny over us. Each in accordance with his own lust is carried away. . . ." [14]

A closer look makes it clear that Melanchthon was reflecting more than Humanism. As we continue to read the lecture, we find both Humanist and Reformer. A classical Humanist put man's own reason against the lusts of his flesh; in contrast, Luther placed the sinful flesh—the whole man—*against the demanding, judging Law of God.* Melanchthon included both:

> There is a strife going on, whether occasioned by reason
> or by Law; in our unhappy state we carry on perpetual
> war with ourselves.[15]

Melanchthon's use of the phrases "strife going on" and "perpetual war with ourselves" was typical Humanist terminology. The body, or flesh, drags man down into sin; the reason, or spirit, struggles upward. One might subdue or dominate the other, but the two are intrinsically opposite. Hence the strife and perpetual war.

On the other hand, Luther's agony as a monk lay in his conviction that his *whole being* was inescapably twisted by sin. No part of his person was untainted. His struggle was not between two parts of his being but in his rebellion against the entrenchment of his being in sin against God. Luther saw "strife" and "perpetual war" within man too. This inward struggle occurs, he taught, when we hear the impossible demands of God's Law and strive in vain to fulfill them. Luther was implacably opposed to any kind of dualism which avoided the extent of man's sin by reducing it to only one part of his being.

A careful examination of Melanchthon's lectures reveals, however, that even as a Humanist he no longer shared this Humanist dualism. As in other instances we are confronted with Humanist language and Reformation intent. There is no suggestion that one half of man is any less sinful than the other. There is no hint that man has a higher nature trying to wrestle free from a lower. Rather we find an unequivocal conviction that sin has enslaved the whole man and that man's reason is powerless to free itself. The deep passions of sin enslave the reason as well as the body, Melanchthon wrote.[16]

The Affections

The clearest evidence of Melanchthon's shift from Humanist to Reformer in the doctrine of sin is found in the section "On the Powers of Man, Especially Free Will," in the *Loci* of 1521. He begins the section with a statement which could also have come from Erasmus: "We divide man into just two parts." [17] But the paragraphs that follow show how he believes that these two parts are both under the crushing dominance of sin.

Melanchthon defines the first part as the "capacity of knowing, by which we perceive, understand and reason"; in short, man's cognition.[18] The second capacity is the "will," "affections," or "appetites." This is the origin of our feelings, emotions, drives, and passions.

Within this framework Melanchthon's argument is three-fold. First, "cognition serves the will"; that is, man's reason is controlled by his will. "For the will in man is just like a tyrant in a republic." [19] With this assertion he repudiates both Scholasticism and Humanism, since both, with variations, supported the supremacy of man's reason. At the same time he agrees with Luther's outlook, which in turn reflects the viewpoint of Nominalism against Rationalism.[20]

Second, the will itself is not sovereign. "For we are convinced by experience and practice that the will cannot bring

forth love, hate, and similar affections by its own power." [21]
These affections lie deep within our being and hold control
over both reason and will.

Melanchthon adds that the categories of reason and will
are unrealistic. The scriptural term "heart" should be used
to designate the most inward being of man, the part of man
which is at the source of all that he is. Man is controlled by
his affections, and these come from his heart.[22]

Third, we ask: What is the nature of the affections? Melanchthon answers:

> The primary and chief affection of human nature is self-
> love, by which it is compelled to desire only those things
> which seem good, agreeable, sweet, and advantageous
> to its own nature.[23]

This self-love is sin itself, "a depraved affection, a depraved
action of the heart against the law of God." [24]

Following Adam's fall the Holy Spirit was no longer an
ever-present guide in man, Melanchthon declares. Man sank
into the darkness of Godless egoism, loving himself more
than God. Since Adam, this condition has been handed down
to all men. This is the sin of our origin, original sin,[25] Melanchthon said, thus abolishing any thought of a distinction
between original and actual sin, a favorite topic of the
Scholastics. Actual sins are simply the fruits of original sin,
he said.

By declaring sin to be a part of man's deepest affections,
Melanchthon also was establishing his belief in "how deeply-
rooted and unfathomable the malice of the human heart
is." [26] He had begun by naming two parts of man, but all

talk of dualism now became unthinkable for him. Both parts, all parts, of man's being are governed from his heart, the center of his affections,[27] he believed.

In the early years of the Reformation the question of the will came to a head in Luther's *The Bondage of the Will,* a massive counterattack against Erasmus, written in 1525. The matter touched the heart of Luther's theology; he argued that since the will and, therefore, the reason were enslaved, man was totally dependent upon God's grace. But where Luther was guarding against an infringement on God's grace, the Humanists feared any trend that would make man less responsible for his actions. Erasmus entered the lists against Luther out of fear that a total "bondage of the will" would be tantamount to declaring that man could aspire to nothing because he was capable of nothing.

Although he affirmed the "bondage of the will" in the *Loci,* declaring that man could not please God in any way but needed his redeeming grace, Melanchthon, as a Humanist, was also uneasy over any hint that man was a puppet, so controlled and bound from above that responsibility was an illusion.[28] He conceded that there was a certain freedom *in external things,* such as what clothes we wear and what we eat for dinner, and he concluded that, while before God man's inner heart and will were bound, in external things he was still a responsible being. This "certain freedom in external acts" later became part of Lutheran theology when Melanchthon reaffirmed it in the *Augsburg Confession,* Article 18.

Natural Knowledge of God

If man lives in darkness without God's Spirit, lost in his sinful affections, we must ask this question: What, then, can natural man know about God? This inquiry introduces us to the whole question of natural theology. This was a critical issue for Melanchthon, if for no other reason than because Humanism and the Reformation flow at cross currents on this topic as well as on others.

In these formative years, however, the problem was not a specific issue. Still feeling his way into the whole discussion, Melanchthon did not deal with the matter explicitly. Nevertheless, he could not escape touching upon it.

In his earliest writings Melanchthon included the admonition to "revere God" among the natural laws.[29] Since natural laws are supposedly those held in common by natural man, whether Christian or not, did this mean that natural man could know God and love him? Melanchthon's initial ambiguity towards this question is best illustrated in the *Loci*, where he mentions "revere God" as a natural law, but then abolishes all possibility of its fulfillment in natural man. According to Romans, Chapter 1, Melanchthon asserts, Paul obviously meant that "God has declared his majesty to all men by the creation and preservation of the universe."[30] But Melanchthon also insists that it is foolish to wonder if man's reason could deduce God's existence. Because of man's condition,

> there is in man a contempt and ignorance of God and whatever other vices described in Psalm 14: The fool has said in his heart, "There is no God."[31]

Certainly, natural man cannot love God. Love comes only from our affections, and,

> these affections are not in our power, so that no one but the spiritually minded can grasp what trust in God, fear of God, and love of God are.[32]

Melanchthon reaffirmed what Luther felt in his pre-Reformation torments. When a man hears God's law and realizes that God judges him as a sinner, he can by no means love God. He can only hate him as a condemning judge.[33]

In his lectures on the Gospel of John, published in 1522-1523, Melanchthon presented his most penetrating analysis of natural man's relationship to God. Here he wrote that sinful man has a concept of God, but he shows why this concept is false and leads man away from true knowledge of God.

In the foreword to this commentary Melanchthon wrote that "since human nature is ignorant of God, it conceives of his image in carnal form." [34] More than anything else, he continued, natural man desires his own glorification. Therefore he wants to be persuaded that he can please God by his own efforts. This "carnal form" of God is one which imagines that God approves of external works. For Melanchthon, as for John, the arrogant self-righteousness of the Pharisees best illustrated this kind of piety.

Natural man, therefore, does not really fear God, Melanchthon believed, since he supposes that his own works are approved by God. He does not love God, for he neither needs him nor depends upon his grace.[35] The Pharisees' attempts to please God ended in nothing but an egoistic self-glorification.

There are other alternatives: Man can reject God altogether,[36] or he can acknowledge God's existence but remain unaffected by him.[37] On the other hand, if he hears the law and takes it seriously, realizing that he is a sinner, he will come to hate God and his judgment.[38] If the self-righteous confidence of sinful man should ever give way to the realization of his inability to obey the law, his fear and despair would repel him from God.[39]

So whatever form this natural knowledge of God takes, it always leads away from God, Melanchthon believed. Natural knowledge of God is not the first step in knowing him, as in the Scholastic scheme. Such knowledge might, and usually does, contain correct ideas about God, but because it is incomplete, it results in self-righteousness, fear, despair, contempt, or simple disregard—all of which finally drive man from God.

From whence, then, does true knowledge of God come? He is revealed not in images which build our self-glorification, but in the event which portrayed the humiliation of the flesh: the cross. God revealed himself in the humiliation of his Son whose death upon the cross signaled the death-sentence of all man's sins as well; to accept Christ as God's revelation means to accept this humiliation of all our pretenses too.

But this, of course, is what sinful flesh and reason abhor doing. Melanchthon wrote: "Reason imagines and desires a Savior who will not condemn the things of the flesh." [40] But

"Christ always appeared to the flesh in a different form, in a different way than the flesh had preconceived." [41] Everything Christ did was an abomination to natural man who prefers a Messiah of pomp and grandeur, because he desires grandeur for himself. Therefore,

> the flesh feels that it is an atrocious indignity to the divine majesty that Christ should demean himself to such an extent that he puts himself in the lowest place. Reason cannot imagine that he is the Lord of glory, he who casts himself down to this, even being made a curse by God.[42]

This is the "scandal of the cross," the reason the cross is offensive to natural man. God revealed himself in such a way that sinful pretensions crumbled. To man, bolstering himself with self-righteousness, this was foolishness, as Paul termed it. "So we come to the knowledge of God through the foolishness of the cross, by making foolish our reason." [43]

This whole concept of God's revelation only in the cross reminds us of Luther's *theologia crucis* ("theology of the cross"). For Luther, too, "Christological knowledge of God, the knowledge of God in Christ, is centered in the cross." [44]

God's revelation must not only overcome the resistance of man's reason; it also does away with any ideas of a free will. Both man's reason and his will are caught in this instinctive rejection of Christ's humiliation. In pointedly, unhumanistic fashion, Melanchthon repeatedly stressed this servitude of the will in his *Annotations,* written only two years before Luther's manifesto *On the Bondage of the Will.*[45] Indeed, Luther was the one who insisted on the publication of this commentary, and one of the reasons for his enthusiasm was Melanchthon's profound analysis of man's inability to accept Christ through his own reason or will.[46]

Man, therefore, can know God only by breaking with his own misconceptions and pretensions. This is accomplished within the framework of the Law and the Gospel. This Law-Gospel structure of God's revelation is evident in the earliest writings of both Luther and Melanchthon and it became basic to all subsequent Lutheran theology.

The Law

Closely related to natural man's knowledge of God (natural theology) is natural man's knowledge of the Law (natural law). Just as Melanchthon seems to be feeling his way into the first topic during these early years, so also is there lack of clarity concerning the Law.

In his Matthew lectures of 1519-1520 Melanchthon defined natural laws in the usual fashion: "Natural laws are particular statements or reflections to which all men assent, just as in human knowledge certain principles are apparent from nature." [47] He listed eight commonly-held, natural laws, such as: revere God, raise children, do not do to others what you do not wish for yourself, share all things with one another, etc.[48] In the *Loci* he summed them up in three laws: revere God, harm nobody, share all things in common.[49]

For evidence of the presence of natural law within man, Melanchthon looked to Paul:

> Paul, in turn, teaches by a marvelously elegant and acute argument in Romans 2:14f. that there is within

us a natural law: In a Gentile there is a conscience
defending or accusing what is done; this is, therefore,
the Law.[50]

But Melanchthon had second thoughts about this: Can
natural man, warped as he is by sin, really come to know the
natural law? He had profound doubts that this was possible.[51] The first of these laws was a special problem. Though
he repeatedly put the law to "revere God" among the
"natural" laws, he also consistently stated that natural man
had, at best, a twisted knowledge of God, and natural man
was incapable of "revering God." [52] What may have been
intended to be a natural law, in other words, is beyond the
capacity of natural man.

Melanchthon might have been unclear in his definition of
the Law, but he was quite clear when he spoke of man's
inability to obey it. Man cannot obey the Law, he said,
whether natural, divine, or moral. Philosophers make their
mistake in thinking that knowing the Law and desiring to
fulfill it are sufficient to obey it. Because sin is so lodged in
our innermost being, we cannot fully obey the Law.[53]

He spoke of natural law and divine law, but any distinction between the two is practically imperceptible. In the
Baccalaureate Theses, for example, they are combined:
"Both divine law and natural law have decreed that God
must be loved for his own sake." [54] Some early passages suggest a distinction between external and internal laws as a
parallel to natural and divine law, but such a distinction is
also not carried through consistently.[55]

In spite of the fact that Melanchthon had not as yet arrived at any final clarity in his thinking, the groundwork for the uses of the Law in later Lutheran theology was being laid. Since natural law implied the intent and content of the Ten Commandments, Melanchthon was leading up to the first use of the Law, the "civil" or "political" use, as it was to be called in later years, by which God created order for human society.

The second and main purpose of the Law was to expose man's inability to obey.

> In truth, God imposed the yoke of the Law upon our shoulders to show us what we are. . . . Therefore the Law should declare sin, coerce, terrify, strike fear in us, and drive us on. . . .[56]

This "use" of the Law was taken, of course, from Paul Both Luther and Melanchthon emphasized it as the chief use of the Law, and it became the "second use" in Lutheran theology. This function of the Law brings man no closer to God. Rather, it has the opposite effect. Melanchthon summed it up in the Baccalaureate Theses:

4. . . . the Law is the reason we fear God in a servile manner.

5. We must hate what we fear.

6. The Law, therefore, causes us even to hate God.[57]

Man is incapable of loving a God who condemns him, he said, although he might try to obey such a God out of fear, not love. The stage was now set for the only means by which this broken fear and hate could be healed—the proclamation of the Gospel, the message of salvation.

Christ's Redemptive Work

It was characteristic of both Luther and Melanchthon that neither ever undertook a logical explanation of Christ's saving work. Salvation in Christ was the cornerstone of the Reformation, constantly affirmed, proclaimed, and preached, but never analyzed in detail. It was the great truth, accepted in faith. In all his *Loci* editions Melanchthon never wrote a section on the "work of Christ," "soteriology," or "redemption." To present the "Christology" of Luther or Melanchthon, one must piece together their thoughts from their writings.

This also means that there is no certain "Reformation Christology." Luther, particularly, uses the fullness of New Testament descriptions and images of Christ in his preaching and writing. Similarities of Christological expression between Luther and Melanchthon can be drawn from many schools of thought—the ancient church, scholasticism, mysticism, humanism, etc. The scholar's task is to determine which of these various viewpoints were most heavily emphasized and to assess the role they played in the individual's theology as a whole.

One's Christology depends upon one's view of sin. The explanation of Christ's work lies largely in the answer to the question: What does he save us from? This viewpoint was particularly true of Melanchthon during his early years. Just as he emphasized different aspects of man's sinful condition, so his portrayal of Christ's mission also took on changing, expanding, shifting colors.

In his first years at Wittenberg, Melanchthon's vision of

Christ was profoundly influenced by the Humanists. As we have noted, the Humanists looked upon man as a creature trapped in his lower, sinful nature, his spirit yearning to be free. Melanchthon never succumbed to the implicit dualism of this concept, but his idea of man was shaped by this thinking.

This view of sin brought Christ's redemptive task into sharp focus: He must make it possible for man to be freed from the tyranny of sin, show how man's spirit should live in harmony with God's spirit, free from fleshly desires. Humanism preached a Christianity attuned to this life on earth. Thoughts of heaven and hell were overshadowed by a Christology geared to earthly life. Christ was "the author of new life"—and that meant new life here and now.

Melanchthon's Humanist heritage is well illustrated in the two of his works already referred to—"Paul and the Scholastics" and the Matthew lectures. In the lecture on Paul he spoke of Christ's twofold work when he wrote that God sent his Son,

> through whom the kingdom of sin and of death might once and for all be destroyed, and in order that law and reason and desire might be brought into conformity therewith.[58]

The promise in Matthew 16:18 (". . . the gates of hell shall not prevail against it.") expresses the Humanist idea of Christ's true mission on earth: "For Christ promises the church universal that by the confession of his name she will defeat hell and abolish her tyranny." [59]

The leading motif of this liberation which Christ won is victory. He has conquered the forces holding us in bondage, and we win victory through him. "Through his victory we have been adopted into sonship. . . . Christ conquered in order that we might conquer in him." [60]

Christ is, therefore, "both example and author of living," Melanchthon said.[61] He is the "exemplar of absolute virtue," the "archetype," and the "author of happiness." [62] He has shown us what true spiritual life is and has helped us achieve it. For the Humanist this was the true purpose of salvation.

Melanchthon and the Humanists were influenced by the theology of the ancient Greek church, especially in the doctrine of the incarnation. One of Athanasius' well-known passages is, "God became man that man might become godly." Melanchthon reflected this same idea when he wrote that the first words of Matthew's Gospel show

> how Christ's incarnation is proclaimed—how God takes on flesh, and we take on God. . . . This is ultimately the absolute incarnation, when we ourselves are made incarnate in the Word.[63]

How familiar Melanchthon was with the ancient Greeks we do not know. But we do know that he had studied the Matthew sermons of the "golden-tongued" St. John Chrysostom, who stood near the end of the ancient Greek tradition.[64] He very likely noticed Chrysostom's comment, "When you hear that God's Son is also the Son af Abraham and David, doubt no longer that you, a son of Adam, will be a son of God." [65] The Greeks, especially Chrysostom, also emphasized the redemption as a liberation and victory.[66]

Comparisons abound, not only with the Humanists and Greeks, but also with Luther, who was fond of using the imagery of Christ the conquering victor and liberator.[67] But where the Humanists were drawn to this language because of their ethical interest in man, it appealed to Luther because of its dramatic and powerful picture of man's enslavement to sin. This, in turn, accentuated the triumphant note in Christ's victory.

How did Christ accomplish this victory? Characteristically, Melanchthon proposed no theory or system of atonement, but a close look at his work reveals that he based the redemption, not on the crucifixion alone, but upon the incarnation as a whole. Christ's earthly life gave us an example of true human life, which the poets and philosophers could not produce.[68]

But Christ was not only an "example"; he was also the "author" of the godly life, opening the way for all men. The key to this Humanist-colored Christology in the Matthew lectures is the account of Christ's temptation by Satan, for Melanchthon summarized Christ's whole mission in this event. Man's predicament is his bondage to Satan and Christ resists Satan, overcoming his tyranny.

> This episode is not intended just as an illustration. Its purpose is this, that, through this victory, we might also be victorious. For all victories, all triumphs of Christ's, belong to all believers. . . . We could not conquer, but for his victory.[69]

This Christology is centered in Christ's ethical perfection.

Redemption is won by his sinless life, Melanchthon said, and the breakthrough to man's salvation lay in the fact that God's Son lived a perfect human life, resisting the assaults of the devil. In such an incarnational Christology the crucifixion plays only a subordinate role. This is typically Humanist, since the Humanists had little use for a sacrificial kind of redemption. Indeed, the Matthew lectures do not include a commentary on the chapters telling of Christ's Passion. But had Melanchthon finished the Gospel, the Humanist-oriented theme of victory and liberation would surely have been carried out.[70]

This lack of any emphasis on Christ's crucifixion and sacrifice in the Matthew lectures is especially significant when we consider the Christology of the *Loci*. Here Christ's incarnation and earthly life, as such, play virtually no role, and redemption now depends exclusively upon the crucifixion.

Far from being an unexpected turn, this change had become inevitable when we consider Melanchthon's deepened view of man's sin. As a Humanist he was concerned with man's ethical life; as a Reformer he saw man's sins and their consequences in terms of God's judgment. He believed man stood not only in bondage to Satan but, above all, under the condemning wrath of God's righteousness. With this shift, Melanchthon had also become "Lutheran," for this was Luther's emphasis. The change also made Melanchthon "Pauline"; he considered the *Loci* primarily as a commentary to Romans.

The verdict of God's judgment is death, he believed. Salvation, therefore, could be accomplished only by carrying out this judgment, and this is what Christ did on the cross.[71] The sacrifices of the Old Testament were prototypes of Christ, who became a sacrifice, victim, expiation, and satisfaction for our sin.[72] Christ was the "author" and "pledge" of our salvation,[73] but in a far different sense than Melanchthon had previously defined.

Within this scheme, Christ's earthly life had little to do with redemption. Of course, it was necessary that his life be sinless, but only as a prerequisite for an effective sacrifice.[74] This conviction of Melanchthon's was in strong contrast to the Matthew lectures, where the sinless life itself was the basis of man's deliverance. Thus one of the most apparent results of Melanchthon's shift from Humanist to Reformer was the change from incarnational to sacrificial Christology.

This change came both from Melanchthon's new conviction of the depth of man's sin and the broadening of his scriptural (especially Pauline) background. It is important to make special note of the Christology of the *Loci*, because it pointed the way toward later *Loci* editions.

But there were problems involved in a sacrificial Christology, of which Melanchthon seemingly was not aware. The main problem concerned the picture of God and the fact that he appeared to have changed from wrath to love on the basis of Christ's sacrifice. God's anger seemed to turn to love only after he was placated with a sacrifice. Melanchthon did, in fact, use this terminology in three passages in the *Loci*. In the section "On Justification and Faith" he wrote, "Moreover, the good will of God was merited by Christ." [75] A few lines farther on he again referred to Christ, "who has earned the mercy of the Father. . . ." [76]

On the basis of these statements alone, God the Father seems to stand apart from the redemptive act of Christ, leading Dr. Rolf Schäfer to charge that Melanchthon had left the Father outside of Christ's work of salvation.[77]

Such a criticism concerned itself, however, with only three passages and ignored the whole context in which Melanchthon spoke. The problem was not that God's initiative and love were missing. It lay, instead, in the fact that any sacrificial Christology ultimately confronted the paradox of God's love and wrath, a paradox which was difficult to reconcile into a logical system. Melanchthon might have developed this sacrificial Christology more logically, but it would have been at the expense of narrowing the concept of God.[78] This he would not do, for the affirmation of God's severe wrath, yet boundless love, formed the cornerstone of his theology.

According to the Loci, Christ did placate God's wrath, but we also find the other side of the paradox, that God the Father was himself moved by love to send his Son to save man. These two sides of God are clearly evident when we consider the first passage in its entirety:

> Moreover, the good will of God was merited by Christ, *whom God gave to us* as a victim and satisfaction.[79]

The loving initiative of the Father, despite his anger against sin, is evident everywhere in the Loci. For example:

> . . . God has given his Son for the confirmation of this trust in him, so that we would not doubt his good will toward us, and so that we would place our hope in him, not forgetting his work. . . .[80]

God's love and initiative are also obvious when we examine two other important concepts, the "promises" and "signs." Immediately after Adam's fall, God gave him a promise of future salvation, the promise of Christ.[81] All through the Old Testament we find promises, "by which God revealed the Gospel right after Adam's fall and then ever more clearly until the time he sent Christ." [82] All these promises point to Christ, the fulfillment of all promises.[83] Behind all of this is the love of God.

Next to the promises are the signs.[84] Throughout the Bible we find signs demonstrating God's grace. Circumcision was the sign of the covenant; Gideon and Hezekiah were given signs in times of crisis (Judges 6, 2 Kings 20). Sacraments can also be called signs, because Baptism and the Lord's Supper are signs which Christ left us.[85] The greatest sign, or sacrament, was Christ himself.[86] All these signs were visible testimonies of God's gracious will. One can hardly speak about a "change of mind or will" in God when one sees all these signs spread out over the centuries.

The impression of God the Father which emerges from the *Loci*, then, is one of love and mercy, out of which Christ was sent. We see one side of God through the Law, namely his wrath, but God is known fully only through the Gospel.[87] Melanchthon might have avoided criticism and misunderstanding by defining this paradox more clearly, but he seems unaware of any great need to do so. Following the phrase "the good will of the Father was merited by Christ" he then quotes John 3:16, a ringing affirmation of God's love.

Luther, on the other hand, sensed the problem and dealt with it extensively, contrasting the opposite sides of God, as

he saw them, in many contexts. He spoke of *deus absconditus* and *deus revelatus,* for example—God hidden and
revealed. He referred to God's work as his *opus alienus* and
opus proprium—his strange or "improper" work (of anger)
and his "proper" work (of love). Thus Luther developed a
more profound concept of God than that which we find in
Melanchthon.

Christ as God's Revelation

The publishing of the *Loci* marked Melanchthon as a
Reformation teacher, but he had by no means achieved a
fully developed outlook. This is especially evident when we
consider his deepening Christology in the *Annotations to
John's Gospel.* Far from having arrived at a final formulation
of Christ's work, he now looked at Christ from an entirely
different standpoint, adding a Johannine note to the Pauline
coloring of the *Loci.* It was basically from these two viewpoints that he approached the Christology of his mature
works.

We have already noted how these *Annotations* furnished a
profound analysis of the *Loci's* teaching concerning man's
predicament. In addition to being under the condemnation
of God for disobedience, man, Melanchthon now explained,
was so blinded by sin that even his most fervent religious
impulses led him farther away from God. The problem was
not only disobedience, but a fundamental ignorance of God.

This broadened view of man in relation to God was reflected in a new dimension of Christology, namely that
Christ was not only a sacrifice, but also God's revelation to

man. Indeed, this is the dominant message of John himself, that the Word of God had become incarnate among men in order that the Father might be made known. Upon this base the whole Christology of this commentary was built. Again and again Melanchthon referred to Christ's reply to Philip, who had asked to be shown the Father: "He who has seen me has seen the Father." [88]

This revelation of God through Christ is the Gospel.[89] Without Christ, man's knowledge of God is related only to the Law—God is just, demands obedience, condemns sins, etc. In these *Annotations,* Melanchthon closely examined the doctrine of Christ as the revelation of the Father, with the language and thought of John as the background. Christ is, above all, the Word of God. Just as our words are expressions of our thought and being, so it is with God.

> For a word is that which represents something else. When God the Father contemplates himself, he conceives an image of himself. This "image" is called the "Word." [90]

With human beings, an image in a mirror or picture is imperfect. The Father's image or word, however, is as perfect as he is.[91] Indeed, the validity of all aspects of Christ's redemptive work rested upon this one fact: Jesus Christ was God. John wrote his Gospel, Melanchthon contended, as a reply to the Ebionites and Gnostics (Cerinthus, Marcion), who denied Christ's full divinity.[92] Melanchthon's exposition of the prologue (John 1:1-18) is a constant emphasis on Christ's divinity. How do we know that Christ's message is true? Melanchthon paraphrased John 8:14: "My testimony is

true, because I am God." [93] Melanchthon also rejected Arius
in strong language, affirming that Jesus was not God "just
by giving him the name of God," but that he was "God by
his very nature." [94]

But how does this sudden "dogmatic" interest in Christ's
divinity compare with Melanchthon's earlier dismissal of all
doctrinal pursuits in favor of simple faith in Christ's "benefits"? Does it mark a return to Scholastic dogmatism, away
from the practical interest in salvation? Not at all. Melanchthon's central concern was still man's redemption through
the "benefits of Christ," but the scope of Christ's benefits
had been widened, including Christ's mission as God's
revelation. In order for these benefits it be valid at all, Christ
must be truly the Son of God, God himself.

Christ's Humiliation

In the *Loci* Melanchthon defined man's sinful situation in
terms of his disobedience to God's law and the condemnation of God's judgment. Over this looms the shadow of the
cross, the sacrifice of Christ, by which God reconciled himself with man. In the *Annotations to John* man's predicament
was defined in terms of his ignorance of God, which drove
him into a false impression of human life. Christ came as
God's revelation, so that man might again know God. This
meant that Christology centered again in the incarnation.
The question now became: What kind of life did the incarnated Word of God live on earth? What did this mean
for the lives of men?

The remarkable thing about the meaning of the incarnation in this commentary was that it was virtually the opposite of the incarnational Christology in the humanistic Matthew lectures. In the earlier lectures the tone of the incarnation was one of triumph, strength, and victory, with Christ coming to earth as a conquering champion of perfection and defeating Satan on the battlefield of temptation. The mood in the lectures on John is also salvation through Christ's life, but through his humiliation and mortification. The keynote is the *mortificatio carnis*, the mortification or humiliation of the flesh.

We have already noted how the main characteristic of the sinful man, the flesh, is the drive to self-glorification. Natural man likes to think that God is on "his side." This, of course, is an illusion, and God must first bring man to his knees in humility. God revealed himself, therefore, in the humiliation of Jesus as his incarnation. Far from coming to earth in pomp and glitter, as men had expected, "Christ brought himself down to the station of the most reproachable man." [95]

This humiliation was thoroughly repugnant to sinful men, and when Jesus claimed his life was his messianic mission from the Father, men were scandalized and cried out, "Crucify him!" The real irony is that the proud men of religion charged the Son of God with blasphemy against God, and this verdict produced the final humiliation on Golgotha when Christ's body was nailed to the cross in shame and indignity. Jesus drew the parallel between his death and the lifting up of the serpent in the wilderness (John 3:14) to show that his crucifixion would be the death of sin.[96]

The sacrificial note of the *Loci* is also present here. John

the Baptist pointed to Jesus and said, "Behold, the lamb of
God" (John 1:29, 36). This, wrote Melanchthon, was "the
sum of the Gospel." [97] Christ was the paschal lamb, the
sacrifice, propitiator, victim, high priest, and satisfaction—
the good shepherd who gave his life for his sheep.[98] Again,
Melanchthon added that Christ's divinity was the foundation
for this aspect of his work. Only a perfect lamb could be a
valid sacrifice in the Old Testament, and Christ was perfect
because he was God.[99] It would be wrong to say that he
brought or taught God's revelation only. He was more than
a prophet or teacher; he was the *effector salutis,* the one who
caused or effected salvation.[100]

The problem in the *Loci* of the Father's "change of mind"
through the sacrifice now fades into the background. Because Christ was God's own Word and revelation, his work
was also the will of the Father.[101] The constant emphasis on
Christ's divinity also emphasized the union of the Father
and the Son, one God, redeeming mankind.

In the Matthew lectures Christ's work was best summarized in the temptation account. In the *Loci* the focal
point was the cross. In the *Annotations to John* the meaning
of the incarnation was best illustrated when Christ washed
the disciples' feet before the Lord's Supper (John 13). "John
begins the account of Christ's passion with this washing"
because this symbolized Christ's passion [102] and expressed
his life's mission: "Christ came down to his own, not for
himself, but that he might wash their feet." [103]

The key to understanding this episode was Christ's conversation with Peter.[104] Here again is the "scandal of the
cross,"

that Peter refuses to let his feet be washed by the Lord ... [because] reason cannot imagine that the Lord of glory would allow himself to sink so low as to be made a curse by God.[105]

But Christ insisted that Peter accept this humiliation, and Peter's reply was the answer of faith: "Lord, not my feet only but also my hands and my head" (John 13:9). This meant that to accept Christ's humiliation was to accept it for ourselves also, marking the end of our pride and self-glorification.[106] Above all, the Christology of this commentary was not only incarnational, but the incarnation became a model of life, a topic which we shall next examine.

Justification and New Life

The Reformation centered in the affirmation of three principles—Grace Alone, Faith Alone, Word Alone. The first two dealt directly with justification. In the first years of the Reformation it was the task of the Reformers to explain justification. But it was equally crucial to define the new life of a justified believer, especially against the earned-righteousness ethics of the Medieval church. How is the Law related to the justified Christian? How could the Reformers steer a middle course between legalism and license? What part do Christ and the Holy Spirit play in the Christian life?

As with other questions, Melanchthon's early years as a Reformer were characterized by a process of searching for and working toward a fully developed expression of these evangelical principles. Various emphases maneuver around

one another with occasional inconsistent frictions and unanswered questions. Once again an examination of the three
early works—the Matthew lectures, the *Loci*, and the *Annotations to John*—furnishes us a picture both of Melanchthon's early development and the thinking which guided his
later theology.

"Grace Alone—Faith Alone" was not a real issue with
Melanchthon in his early years as a Reformer. In their own
way the Humanists also affirmed this twofold truth.[107]
Erasmus, as well as Luther, was thoroughly Christ-centered
in this concept of salvation.[108] This Christocentricity was also
predominant in Melanchthon's Matthew lectures: "For
Christ alone is righteousness, life, peace and truth." [109] Only
in Christ can man break the bondage which enslaves him.

This salvation is only through faith, Melanchthon believed.
"This much stands fast: Faith is the basis of our justification." [110] Melanchthon also anticipated his later teaching by
equating faith with trust.[111] But in the Matthew lectures,
faith was not only the "basis" but, more specifically, the
"beginning" of salvation.[112] Justification is a process begun
by faith, when we accept in faith Christ's victory over evil.
This is described by Melanchthon as an "enrapturing" (*raptus*): We are seized by the Holy Spirit, by whose power our
sinful affections are overcome, and freed to live pure lives.

> Christ came for no other reason than to bestow the
> Spirit, by whom our souls are enraptured and trans-
> formed to embrace heavenly things. . . .[113]

Since the Humanists were so concerned about ethical life
and universal, natural, and moral law, it is natural that

Melanchthon should term this "rapture" a turning from the lusts of the flesh to obedience to the Law. Christ's work embraced both aspects: "Indeed, when Christ was incarnated, both the means for doing the law and the forgiveness of sins became manifestly known." [114] It is in this way that "Christ justifies us through his Spirit." [115]

Therefore justification is, above all, this new capacity for obedience to the Law. It is begun in faith but is really a continuous process. Righteousness is not pronounced or imputed but actually effected within us. Melanchthon speaks of "the righteousness of Christ, which Christ works in us." [116]

The purpose of justification is thus our fulfillment of the Law. We, of course, never attain this perfectly, but our remaining imperfection is not condemned. For that we are forgiven. This is how Melanchthon interpreted the passage in Matthew 5:17 which declares: "I have not come to abolish the law and the prophets, but to fulfill them." Melanchthon wrote:

> Christ gives the Spirit, through whom our affections are changed and enraptured to do the Law. Whatever is transgressed after that is forgiven by taking refuge in Christ through his name. Thus Christ fulfills the Law.[117]

To be sure, justification takes place "by grace alone," or "in Christ alone," and "by faith alone," but the weight is clearly on the obedience of the Law.[118]

This early Humanist-colored doctrine of justification stands in marked contrast with Luther. This difference is best illustrated in Luther's *Galatians Commentary* of 1519,

a work which Melanchthon very likely had studied before
or during the preparation of his Matthew lectures.[119] Luther
used some of the same language as Melanchthon. For example: ". . . righteousness and the fulfilling of the Law have
been begun through faith. . . ."[120] But Melanchthon had
implied that our works fulfill the Law, with Christ's righteousness "covering" only our remaining sin. Luther, on the
other hand, was quite explicit, declaring that both our
righteousness and the fulfillment of the Law are Christ's.
Our works are not done as a saving fulfillment of the Law;
they are rather a consequence of the fulfillment we already
have by faith in Christ.[121] Basic to Luther's concept was this
statement:

> The apostle's rule is this: It is not works that fulfill the
> Law, but the fulfillment of the Law produces works.
> One does not become righteous by doing righteous
> deeds. No, one does righteous deeds after becoming
> righteous. Righteousness and fulfillment of the Law
> come first, before the works are done, because the latter
> flow out of the former.[122]

Luther was all too conscious of the depth of man's sin and
knew that this sin burdened even believers, in contrast to the
rather naive ethical optimism of the Humanists. In his
Galatians Commentary he expressed this realistic outlook
with the two formulas which became distinctive in his
theology—neither of which Melanchthon explained as well.
First, the Christian is *simul iustus, simul peccator,* "simultaneously righteous and sinful."[123] Since sin always remains,

one cannot speak of perfection in man's works. Secondly, believers are righteous *nondum plene in re sed in spe:* "not yet fully in fact, but in hope." [124] Our righteousness lies not in actual deeds, but in faith and hope. This Reformation insight was not affirmed by Melanchthon until he abandoned the Humanist traces in his teachings of sin and justification.

These Humanist influences were virtually eliminated in the next few years, but the basic question concerning the place of the Law in a believer's life occupied Melanchthon throughout his life. For a radically different viewpoint, we now turn to the *Loci,* where we meet Melanchthon the Reformer. No longer is righteousness a quality which the "justifying spirit" works within us. In the section "On Justification and Faith" he begins:

> We are therefore justified when, after being mortified through the Law, we are lifted up by the word of grace, promised in Christ, and by the Gospel which forgives sins. To Christ we cling in faith, being certain that his righteousness is ours, that his satisfaction is our expiation, and that his resurrection is ours.[125]

We can trace the young professor's path to this Reformation doctrine of justification by examining two passages in the *Loci* which show traces of his earlier ideas. First: "For justification has begun but is not consummated." [126] Second: "Now here we have begun to be justified, but this justification is not finished." [127] These statements do not sound like those of a Reformer, but an examination of their contexts reveals that evangelical insights have drastically altered Melanchthon's early thinking.

In the section on justification Melanchthon dealt with the works which followed justification, the same works which established our righteousness in the Matthew lectures. Now Melanchthon reversed himself. These works, "done in yet impure flesh are even themselves impure." [128] The first passage—that justification "is not consummated"—was set in this context. Here "justification" was used in its previous sense of ethical righteousness, but Melanchthon made it clear that this kind of justification was unattainable: Man can never be justified by his works.

The second passage was set in a similar context "concerning the sins of the saints or the remains of the old man in the regenerated." [129] Melanchthon declared that the subject of sin remaining in saints had been sufficiently treated by Paul, Cyprian, Augustine, and Luther,[130] and then simply asserted that in this sense our justification had only begun. Again, the word *justificare* was used in an ethical, Humanist sense, showing that such justification was unreachable. Melanchthon continued by arguing that justification therefore could be neither by works nor by law.[131] Just as circumcision did not justify in Paul's time, so none of our works justify either. Melanchthon concluded by affirming the Reformation truth: "Therefore, faith alone justifies, as Paul says, 'The just shall live by faith.'" [132]

In both passages the word *justificatio* was used in its earlier, Humanist sense, but the contexts made it clear that this ethical sense had come to an impasse.[133] In this shift, Melanchthon emerged as a Reformer. Four factors led to this new doctrine of justification:

(1) As we have noted, salvation was now concerned first and foremost with man's sins and his disobedience of God's law, rather than simply with his ethical life. In addition, Melanchthon saw clearly that man could never rid himself of sin; he had grasped Luther's *simul iustus et peccator,* though he himself never used the term. Our righteousness, therefore, could never come from our works, but only from Christ.

(2) Furthermore, the idea of justification by works was not only impossible, but it destroyed faith itself by placing trust in ourselves instead of Christ.[134] This was the mistake of much of Scholastic and Roman Catholic piety with all its talk about merits.

(3) Grace was no longer confused with the workings of the Holy Spirit. It was the *favor dei,* God's favor, benevolence, or mercy.[135] Justification as the reception of God's grace was, therefore, not the ethical renewal itself, but rather the reception of God's mercy through faith.[136] Because God's grace was expressed primarily in the forgiveness of sins, this forgiveness now began to be predominant in Melanchthon's doctrine of justification.[137]

(4) By defining faith as "trust" *(fiducia),* Melanchthon undercut the intricacies of Scholastic quibbling.[138] Since trust was quite different from merits or works on our part, justification could not be confused with them.[139] Faith was not something which justified but an attitude

toward God through which his righteousness was received.

These new insights combined to produce a Reformation teaching of justification in the *Loci*. We are saved by grace alone, that is, God's favor or mercy. Since we are justified by God's grace, "justification is attributed to faith alone, for only by faith do we receive God's promised mercy."[140] Therefore we are righteous through faith, for "Christ's righteousness is our righteousness through faith."[141]

It is interesting to note that in this first *Loci* Melanchthon never used the term "imputation" *(imputatio)* of Christ's righteousness. In the Matthew lectures he was far from such a thought, but the essence of the idea is present in the *Loci*, though the word did not become the standard description of justification until later.[142] In 1519-1520 neither Luther nor Melanchthon used the word.[143] Although Luther does not specifically mention *imputatio,* he does speak of "another's righteousness" *(justitia aliena)* which is essentially the same as "imputed" righteousness.[144] However, Melanchthon does use the related word *reputare:*

> . . . righteousness is revealed in this way, that God reputes as righteousness that which is through faith in Jesus Christ.[145]

The absence of *imputatio* illustrates how the *Loci* represents an early state of Melanchthon's development as a Reformer. The word "justification" was used in its earlier sense, but the threshold into Reformation thinking has been crossed. The evangelical truth is clearly proclaimed. "Christ's righteousness is ours . . . Christ's satisfaction is our expiation. . . . Righteousness is faith alone in God's mercy and grace in Jesus Christ." [146] In the years to come this path would lead him to his "mature" Reformation theology.

Free from the Law

Being justified by grace through faith, we are freed from the Law, according to Melanchthon's Reformation outlook in the *Loci*. But the young professor had not yet really decided what relevance the Law had for the Christian. His Humanist concept—that justification was precisely our capacity to do the Law—was dropped. Yet the Reformers were certainly not willing to abandon the Law altogether. Thus we find an uneasy ambiguity in this first *Loci*.

First of all, the Law could no longer condemn.[147] The whole Law—judicial, ceremonial, and moral—had been abrogated as a judge against man.[148] In this sense Melanchthon said, "it must even be acknowledged that the Decalogue has been antiquated." [149]

But any suggestion of antinomian libertinism was instinctively abhorrent to Melanchthon's temperament. True faith results in renewed lives. Melanchthon concluded that this took place automatically because God's Spirit led us to do his will.[150]

They who have been renewed by the Spirit of Christ will of their own accord—even without the demands of the Law—be compelled to do that which the Law commands.[151]

Therefore Christian liberty and freedom from the law simply meant that "we will and wish spontaneously in our hearts whatever the Law demands." [152]

Melanchthon was realistic enough to know that man's continuing sinfulness would plague any such "spontaneous" fulfillment of the Law, so he qualified himself by asserting that "only the new man is free." [153] This led him to the logical, though certainly awkward conclusion: "So we are free insofar as we have been renewed by the Spirit, but insofar as we are flesh and the old man, we are under the law. . . ." [154] The implication of this two-sided concept is obvious: Freedom from the Law is theologically true, but from a practical and ethical standpoint, it is somewhat unworkable. The believer is still tainted with sin, so that the Law is always relevant, not to condemn but to guide. This ambiguity in the *Loci* eventually gave way to Melanchthon's (and the Lutheran church's) teaching of the *tertius usus legis,* the "third use of the law." [155]

One cannot help noticing in the *Loci* that Christian ethics are oriented around the Law, not the life of Christ as an example. Indeed, we have already seen how the *Loci* dealt with the incarnation only incidentally, centering almost exclusively on the cross. But this is not to say that Christ has nothing to do with the Christian's life. We are able to follow the Law because God's Spirit dwells within us, and this is synonymous with the presence of Christ. Melanchthon spoke often of the "Spirit of Christ." [156] Faith is the reception of the *spiritus Christi,* which leads us into renewed living. This term makes it evident that Melanchthon did not consider justification and sanctification as two separate topics, but as an organic whole, one flowing into another, through the work of the "Spirit of Christ."

The Knowledge of Christ

When Melanchthon worked through the Gospel of John after the *Loci,* he concentrated especially on Christ's mission as revelation of the Word to a world blinded by ignorance. Justification and righteousness came, first of all, from true knowledge of God, which is through Christ. For this reason, Melanchthon constantly stressed that "the sum of justification is the knowledge of Christ. . . ." [157] In the same way, "this knowledge of Christ is righteousness." [158] Therefore "faith alone is righteousness," since this knowledge is synonymous with faith and trust.[159]

In his exposition of the conversation between Jesus and Nicodemus, Melanchthon began to draw out the consequences of his previous teaching in the *Loci;* he explained how Christ's righteousness is "communicated" to us by imputation.

> Finally, Christ teaches us that we must be reborn and shows us through whom we are reborn, and whose righteousness is imputed to us for salvation.[160]

The term *imputare* was used only in this framework of the Nicodemus conversation,[161] but it indicates again the direction in which the *Loci* was pointed.

The fact that this *imputatio-imputare* was set in the context of Jesus' admonition to Nicodemus, that we must be "born again," shows how justification and regeneration are intimately related, if not indeed synonymous. This "knowledge of Christ" is that which justifies, regenerates, and renews us—all inseparably. Jesus proclaimed the Word, so that

> the hearing of this Word is justification, and the power of this Word is to save, effect truth, establish a new light, and enlighten darkness.[162]

This gave Melanchthon a dynamic, inclusive view of justification. Since justification and regeneration both come from this "knowledge of Christ" in faith, he could even write, "Christ says that justification is regeneration, that is, that the flesh is truly mortified and renewed by the Spirit." [163] Justification itself is the "communication" or "imputation" of Christ's righteousness to us, which is precisely what also regenerates and renews us.

The renewed life which Christ works in us is described in the *Annotations to John* in a radically different fashion than in the *Loci*. The *Loci* pictured the Christian life in terms of the Law, which the "Spirit of Christ" produced. In the *Annotations* the pattern was not the Law but the life of Christ himself. He came to earth and mortified his flesh and, in doing so, revealed the way for our lives.[164]

This was why Christ washed the disciples' feet. He humbled himself to serve them and love them, showing them the path they too should follow. The commandment to love our neighbor means that we "cast ourselves among all people, renouncing all status, honor, even life." [165] This is what it is to deny oneself and take up Christ's cross.[166] This is precisely what the Pharisees would never do.

To describe the life of a follower of Christ, Melanchthon used the term "afflictions" *(afflictiones).* We might suffer afflictions, but though this is the will of God, our faith can be strengthened by knowing that he steadfastly helps us.[167]

Just as the Christian's mortification and afflictions come from Christ, so also does his hope. Christ's crucifixion was followed by his resurrection. In the same way, our mortification and afflictions are succeeded by glorification. The cross brings eternal life also for us, an eternal life which can come only by taking the cross.

> Because sin must be washed away by death, eternal life must be the life of the cross. Christ commends this, therefore, by his example. so that we might know that death is the instrument by which we are glorified.[168]

By following Christ we become "sons of God by adoption." [169] Melanchthon expressed this in a passage reminiscent of ancient Greek Christology, reflecting also his earlier Matthew lectures:

> So now John (1:14) speaks of the incarnation, putting it in its proper perspective: As in Christ the Word was made flesh, so also must the Word become flesh in us. That is rebirth.[170]

Melanchthon summarized his view of our relation to

Christ with the oft-repeated sentence: "For we must conform to Christ's image.[171] From the standpoint of Melanchthon's later development, this conception of the Christian life was remarkable in two ways. First, the Christology
was thoroughly incarnational, not only in redemption but
even more so in an ethical sense. In his life Christ showed
us how to live. While Melanchthon did not use the phrase
"imitation of Christ," he shared much in common with the
idea of Christ as our example. In sharp contrast to the *Loci*,
where the incarnation had nothing to do with Christian
living, Melanchthon here sounds much like Luther. Though
Luther also avoided an explicit "imitation of Christ" viewpoint, he did look to Christ as an example. According to
Luther, "the Christian should take on the same form as his
Lord, Jesus Christ." [172]

Second, Melanchthon's commentary on John reveals a
close parallel to Luther's "theology of the cross." Bernhard
Lohse described Luther's opinion: "Indeed, the life of a
Christian does not just signify the cross of Christ, but is
itself the cross of Christ." [173] Luther wrote in his Galatians
commentary: "It is necessary that we be destroyed and
rendered formless, in order that Christ may be formed and
be alone in us." [174]

There is also a strong similarity between Melanchthon's
idea of a Christian's "afflictions" and Luther's *Anfechtungen*,
his struggles and torments.[175] Prof. Walther von Loewenich
says that "according to Luther the true Christian inevitably
draws the hostility of the world upon himself, so that hard-
ship might well be inescapable." [176] Like Melanchthon,

Luther stressed the polarities in John's Gospel—God—world, Christ—Satan, light—blindness.[177] The Christian finds himself opposed and rebuked. Both Luther and Melanchthon saw God's will behind these afflictions, but looked to him for help and strength. Here, again, Luther explained this paradox, in part, with his categories of *deus absconditus* and *revelatus*, whereas Melanchthon did not analyze it further.

Both Luther and Melanchthon referred to Christ as our "example" *(exemplum)*. Melanchthon's use of the word was similar to the English meaning. This was the Humanist understanding, that Christ was the supreme example of ethical perfection toward which we too aspire.[178] In the *Annotations to John,* Melanchthon wrote that it was Christ's life of humiliation and mortification which became the example or pattern for our life. Luther's concept of Christ as example emphasized Christ more as an archetype who became united with us.

Luther's idea of the unity of Christ and the believer *(Gemeinschaft Christi, communio Christi)* played a far greater role in his theology than in Melanchthon's. Melanchthon spoke of Christ working in us and giving us his righteousness, whereas Luther constantly pointed to the fact that the person of Christ and the believer had become joined together.[179] But in spite of this difference, Melanchthon displays more similarity to Luther in this commentary to John than in any other writing.[180]

Special notice must be given to the fact that in the *Annotations to John* the Law played no role whatsoever in the Christian life, making this book unique among Melanchthon's writings. The Christian life is oriented wholly around Christ's life, not the Law. It is, of course, consistent with the Law, but the Law is not at all the basis of Christian ethics. This is remarkable, not only in view of Melanchthon's previous work, but especially as we consider his later development toward the "third use" of the Law.

The Church and Eternal Life

In his early years as a Reformer, Melanchthon had little to say about either of these topics. It was really not surprising, however, that he wrote very little about eschatology, or eternal life, since both Humanists and Reformers dealt primarily with the immediate situation.[181] Eternal life was of course affirmed, but the real problems were the polemical issues of sin, justification, etc. From his Humanist background, Melanchthon also tended instinctively toward the practical and present aspects of evangelical doctrine, looking for renewal in the Christian here and now.

When we consider the situation of the early 1520's, Melanchthon's lack of ecclesiology, a doctrine of the church, was also understandable. The Humanists concentrated upon individual piety and looked upon the institutional church with skepticism.[182] The Reformer's view of the church was dominated by the frontal assault of Luther's *Babylonian Captivity,* and they did not have time to work out an evangelical doctrine of the church. Because of his ecclesiastical background as a monk and his position as the natural leader in reorganizing church life, Luther was far more concerned with this issue than the academic Melanchthon. It was not until the turn of the decade, at the Diet of Augsburg, that Melanchthon really came to grips with formulating a statement about the church.

When we deal with the sacraments, however, we find that Melanchthon had more to say. Luther had defined the evangelical position with forceful vigor in the *Babylonian Captivity*, a document which Melanchthon accepted with enthusiasm.[183] Nonetheless, his background and outlook gave his views a flavor of their own. Humanism did not bequeath to him a "sacramental" piety. Humanist faith concentrated on Christ-centered, renewed living, not ecclesiastical ceremonies. It was not so dependent upon the church as the spender of sacramental grace. Thus Melanchthon's whole point of view was different from that of Luther, a priest whose life and piety had been immersed in the structure and rites of the church. One of the obvious indications of this difference was that Melanchthon abandoned the doctrine of transubstantiation much earlier than Luther.

Melanchthon understood the sacraments within the framework of Law and Gospel. In the *Loci* the sacraments are dealt with in the section "On Signs." The signs, in turn, were the means by which God revealed his gracious will, that is, the Gospel. A sacrament was a sign, just as circumcision was a sign to Abraham, the fleece to Gideon, or the shadow to Hezekiah. The visible sign was added to a promise, and being visible, its purpose was to arouse and strengthen faith.[184] In this sense, Christ himself was a sacrament, since his life and death were visible testimonies of God's grace and the forgiveness of sins.[185]

In Baptism water "signifies a passing through death into
life, the immersing of the old Adam into death and the
emerging of the new man." [186] It means that vivification follows mortification and that throughout our entire life the
old man must constantly be put to death so that the new
man can come forth. Baptism is, therefore, not an isolated
initiation rite but the Gospel sign which embraces our continual repentance and renewal, an emphasis also of Luther's.

The Lord's Supper is also a visible sign of God's forgiveness. Since the mode of Christ's presence in the Eucharist
had not yet become a critical question, Melanchthon simply
affirmed that in the sacrament we "eat Christ's body and
drink his blood," without defining it further. His great concern, however, was to clarify the purpose of the Lord's
Supper. The Roman Catholic idea of the sacrament as a
sacrifice offered by us for merits was abhorrent to him.
Rather, "the meaning of this sacrament is to confirm us as
often as our consciences falter, or as often as we doubt God's
will toward us." [187] Melanchthon's lack of interest in eucha-
ristic dogma and his concern for the purpose of the Lord's
Supper set the direction for his future years.

A survey of Melanchthon's early writings reveals that
many currents and ideas were swirling about in his thinking.
These were the years of the Reformation "breakthrough,"
and in the coming years the loose ends will be brought
together and formed into a coherent whole. The decade of
the 1520's will be a period of reappraisal, confronting
the wider problems involved in restoring church life according to evangelical truths. This period in Melanchthon's

life reaches a climax in the summer of 1530, when he works to formulate the Augsburg Confession, the first "official" statement of the Reformation church. The congress at Augsburg marks the watershed for Melanchthon, since after that he goes on to crystallize his "mature" theology in the later *Loci* editions and other documents.

CHAPTER TWO

Spokesman

The Reformation began as a protest against the Roman Catholic Church. Within a short time, however, the Wittenberg Reformers were faced with a bewildering variety of other evangelical groups.

The storm broke in 1521 during Luther's protective custody in the Wartburg Castle. Andrew Karlstadt, Thomas Münzer, and the "Enthusiasts" took over the town. With fiery self-confidence that the Holy Spirit personally led them, they began their campaign of iconoclastic destruction and innovation. Melanchthon was somewhat taken aback by their claims, and as the weeks went by he grew to oppose and violently dislike their entire movement. However, it was too much for a 24-year-old professor to put a stop to the blaze. Luther himself had to extinguish it by returning to Wittenberg in the spring of 1522.

Both Luther and Melanchthon considered the radical Reformation "on the left" as detrimental as the abuses of the Roman Church, if not more so. The radicals not only held church history, traditions, and culture in contempt in their restoration of "pure" Christianity, but they also tended to give their own arbitrary, "spirit-inspired" ideas precedence over the written word of Scripture. Since the splintering of the Reformation churches took some almost bizarre directions, Melanchthon's later *Loci* editions were strongly shaped by his reactions to these extremes.

Luther, of course, was the undisputed leader of the Wittenberg Reformers, but with the publication of the first *Loci*, Melanchthon emerged as their spokesman. Luther himself admired the young professor's literary talents and encouraged him to turn his attention exclusively to theology, but Melanchthon insisted on remaining a teacher of Greek. As it turned out, he carried an extra heavy load, teaching Greek, holding regular theological lectures, and writing constantly.

Years of Activity

The decade following the *Annotations to John*, from about 1523 to 1533, was the formative period for Melanchthon's theology. During this time the new insights were sifted, crystallized, and applied to church life. The various currents flowing in his early works now began to fall into place. The front widened, so that he had to address himself not only to the Roman Church on the right and the Enthusiasts on the left, but to the Zwinglians (later the Calvinists) in Switzerland, the South German evangelicals, and the academic community in general.

These years were packed with feverish activity—lecturing, advising, writing, traveling, negotiating. A complete account of all this would fill another volume, but there are certain highlights which illustrate Melanchthon's emergence as a Reformation teacher and spokesman.

While traveling through Southwest Germany in 1524, Melanchthon met the young Landgraf Philip of Hesse. The 20-year-old count asked Melanchthon to explain the evangelical faith, and he responded by writing an *Epitome of the Restored Church Doctrine* when he returned to Wittenberg.[188]

In the *Epitome* he described the terrified conscience being lifted up by faith in Christ, who made satisfaction for our sins. The righteousness of faith was contrasted with the human righteousness of law and reason. Since the radicals rejected almost all church traditions, the *Epitome* concluded by discussing traditions, asserting that the Reformers reject only those traditions which expressly lead to sin.

Soon after he read the *Epitome*, Count Philip joined the Reformation, becoming a life-long staunch but temperamental supporter. His friendship with Melanchthon, begun on a country road, became a warm and long-standing bond.

The crucial focal point of the Reformation was not in the monasteries, universities, or even the princely castles. Ultimately it had to become real in the congregational life of the people. The decade of the 1520's saw the Reformers immersed in the practical tasks of bringing these evangelical teachings to the parishes. This was especially true of Luther. After finishing his German translation of the New Testament at Wartburg, he began translating the Old Testament; he formulated German liturgical services and worship instructions; in 1524 he produced a book of 23 hymns, which made singing such a mark of evangelical worship; in 1529 he published the Large and Small Catechisms.

But what *was* the situation in Saxon congregations? At

Luther's urging, Elector John the Steadfast commissioned Melanchthon to visit Saxon churches. In the summer of 1527 Melanchthon traveled through Thuringia in southern Saxony. He was appalled at the chaos he encountered. Roman practices, Enthusiast overtones, and clerical ignorance were all jumbled together. There was no harmony or consistency whatsoever.

Melanchthon remained at Jena in Thuringia during the fall and winter of 1527 and 1528 to avoid the plague epidemic in Wittenberg. With the impressions of the visitation fresh in his mind, he compiled the "Visitation Articles." [189] In short, clear paragraphs he outlined doctrinal and practical issues as a guide for church instruction and order. The thought behind the articles concerned the Law and the Gospel: Faith must be preceded by true repentance, which is incited by the Law, a fear of God's judgment. Justification is through faith in Christ, and this is followed by the fruits of the Spirit. Obviously, Melanchthon had missed a sense of genuine repentance in men's souls among the churches.

Other topics dealt with in the "Visitation Articles" were the cross, prayer, civil magistrates, the sacraments, marriage, human traditions, Christian freedom, and free will. Luther and John Bugenhagen approved the articles, and the Elector made them the basis for worship in the Saxon churches.

In January 1530 Emperor Charles V summoned German rulers to an Imperial Congress (Diet) at Augsburg, hoping to resolve the religious crisis. At Elector John's request, Melanchthon and other theologians met at Torgau in March to prepare for the meeting. Melanchthon presented the

elector with the "Torgau Articles," more than 20 articles
dealing chiefly with abuses in the Roman Catholic Church.[190]

The elector asked Melanchthon to formulate the evangelical teachings. In addition to the "Torgau Articles" Melanchthon took with him to Augsburg the "Schwabach
Articles." [191] These articles had been written in 1529 as a
basis of united faith between Saxony, Brandenburg-Ansbach,
and the city of Nürnberg. Here, again, Melanchthon was
the chief author, though certainly in close collaboration with
Luther and others.

Mention should also be made of the "Marburg Articles,"
the result of a meeting of Luther and Melanchthon with
the Zwinglians in October 1529. This meeting cleared up
much misunderstanding, but blocking complete harmony
was the unresolved disagreement about the Lord's Supper.

Carrying these documents, Melanchthon and the Witten-
bergers made their way to Augsburg. Luther, branded as a
"wanted—dead or alive" outlaw, could venture no farther
than Coburg, the southernmost outpost of Saxony. Arriving
in Augsburg, the Saxons were shocked to learn that Dr. John
Eck, Luther's 1519 debate opponent from Leipzig, had
widely circulated his "404 Articles." These were a vitriolic
attack on all the Protestants, lumping together the Wittenberg Reformers and the radical extremists and accusing
them of all sorts of ancient and modern heresies. With this
sensational attack on everybody's mind, it became necessary
to write a document specifically for this occasion.

Melanchthon's task in Augsburg was, therefore, twofold:

1. He must show the emperor that the "Lutherans" were

trying to restore the ancient teachings, not destroy them. He must emphasize that the Reformers built their doctrine upon the Scriptures and church fathers. The evangelical church was the true "catholic" church, restoring the apostolic faith.

2. Melanchthon must establish that it was, in fact, the Roman church which deviated from the ancient, scriptural faith. Religious peace could be reached only when the whole church was reformed in accord with evangelical truth.

Melanchthon labored in Augsburg through the spring of 1530. Much of his time was spent in lengthy and exhausting consultation with evangelical princes and theologians. The Torgau and Schwabach Articles provided a background, but Melanchthon wished to compile a brief but more comprehensive statement of evangelical convictions. There was continual correspondence with Luther in Coburg, and from his castle room there Luther gave Melanchthon's final *Confession* his full approval.

The climax came on June 25, 1530, when the *Augsburg Confession* was read to the emperor—who, observers later wrote, was bored by the momentous event and dozed off occasionally.

The *Confession* was a milestone both in Melanchthon's career and in his theology. It was the high point of his life's work until then, since the *Confession* became the first official statement of evangelical beliefs. For Melanchthon personally his earlier theology was summarized in the *Confession*. Indeed, Melanchthon later would even take the liberty of amending the *Confession* on his own, since he regarded it as his own confession as well as the church's. From this watershed his later "mature" theology would now flow, beginning immediately with his *Apology to the Confession* in 1531, his *Romans Commentary* of 1532, and his second *Loci* edition of 1535.

Concern About Doctrine

During this decade Melanchthon's life-work became clear: to explain, clarify, and defend the Reformation faith.

The fundamental difference between Luther and Melanchthon was more of style than of content. Luther was a preacher; Melanchthon was a teacher. Luther's language was imaginative, vivid, and dramatic; Melanchthon's was precise and explicit. Luther spoke expansively; Melanchthon defined, outlined, and summarized his topic.

Reading Luther, one is struck by this colorful imagery and dramatic flair, and how impossible it is to condense Luther into a consensus of doctrinal statements. It is no wonder that there is a different "theology of Luther" for every theologian who presents it.

Reading Melanchthon is an entirely different experience. Researchers might discuss some varying interpretations, but the main body of his thought is quite distinctly understood. In his endeavor to be absolutely clear he often repeats himself to the point of monotony, circumscribing every possible aspect of a topic. His *Apology* explanation of justification or the 1532 *Romans Commentary* furnish good examples of this.

Consequently, he was often accused of "intellectualizing"

theology by overemphasizing the importance of "pure doctrine." He was, his critics charge, laying the foundation for
the sterility of the "Age of Orthodoxy." This charge deserves
a second look.

To be sure, Melanchthon was an "intellectual," a precise
and exacting thinker who made up in clarity what he lacked
of Luther's dramatic impact. True, his life-long concern was
with doctrine, but it is also true that a crucial task of the
time was the need to clarify Reformation beliefs, and this
job fell to Melanchthon. The young church continually
looked to him for formulations and definitions, and he was,
in Luther's own opinion, the man superbly fitted for the
task. If he laid heavy emphasis on doctrine, it was in response to the immediate needs of his church.

But nowhere did Melanchthon equate faith with doctrinal
knowledge; for him the central note of faith was always
trust—reliance upon Jesus Christ as Savior. The knowledge
to which faith clings is the simple Gospel message of the
cross and resurrection, not a complex theological system.

Melanchthon was accused also of thinning down and
diluting the richness of Luther's broad vision. This was
partially true and perhaps inevitable. His task, after all, was
to present the Reformation case simply and understandably.
To do this, he was bound to emphasize some of Luther's
insights more than others, as we shall see. He naturally
brought those things to the fore which he considered valuable and which, in his opinion, contributed most to a clear
understanding of the Gospel. Luther, above all, appreciated
Melanchthon's skill in summarizing the evangelical faith.

It is obvious that in articulating doctrine, Melanchthon

simplified and condensed much of what Luther said. The
most obvious illustration of this is found in their respective
views of Jesus Christ.

For Luther, the preacher, the Gospel *was* Jesus Christ. Luther loved to preach on all aspects of Christ's life: His birth
was an example of humility; the care from his parents was a
pattern for all parents; his knowledge of the Scriptures an
inspiration for all of us to study; his calling of the disciples
a call to us; his controversies with the Pharisees a warning
against legalism; his life the perfect example of human
life; his suffering and death for our salvation. "We are
Christs and Christ's, both nominative and genitive," [192] Luther said. Theologians and scholars have rightly marveled
at the rich and profound Christology of Luther.

Melanchthon, the teacher, striving for everyone to see
clearly the Reformation message of salvation by grace, concentrated primarily on Christ's saving work, his death and
resurrection. This strong emphasis on justification caused
him to focus, above all, on the cross. The other elements of
Christ's life became subordinate to this overwhelming event.
The Christology of the first *Loci* set the tone for his later
theology. The emphasis on the incarnation in the Matthew
and John lectures faded into the background.[193]

Another shift was that the Gospel was not so much Christ
himself, but the truth or Gospel *about* Christ, the proclamation of Christ's saving work on the cross. Luther dwelt on
the person of Christ, Melanchthon on Christ's work. Luther
liked to speak about the Christian's personal union and
fellowship with Christ; Melanchthon wrote about Christ
more as the one who won for us our salvation. These con-

trasts did not represent contradictory views or a disagreement between the two men. Rather, they reflected two
views of the same thing, or two different contexts in which
their thoughts moved.

A remarkable example of this difference can be seen in a
letter which Melanchthon wrote to Johannes Brenz in May
1531, to which Luther affixed a postscript. The Reformers
felt that Brenz still harbored the Roman Catholic notion
that justification depended also on the works of law and
obedience, rather than on faith alone. They wished to make
clear that righteousness comes wholly from Christ. Melanchthon wrote:

> . . . you must direct your attention to Christ's promise,
> in order that you may see that it is for Christ's sake
> and not because of this renewal that we are righteous.
> . . . We are, therefore, righteous by faith alone, not
> because, as you express yourself, it is the root of our
> renewal, but because it is directed to Christ. It is be-
> cause of him that we are acceptable to God. . . . We are
> therefore righteous . . . because in faith we lay hold of
> Christ. . . ." [194]

Christ is clearly the basis of our salvation, Melanchthon
was saying. We are accepted by God because of his work.
In Luther's postscript, Christ is not only the basis of our
righteousness, but he himself, *as a person in us,* is our
salvation:

> . . . I make it a rule to remind myself that there is in
> my heart no quality of any kind that could be called
> faith or love. But I put in their stead Jesus Christ and

say: There is my righteousness . . . I understand him
to be the one who is *in and by himself* what he teaches
me and gives me as his gift. I, therefore, have everything. Remember that he himself says: "I am the way,
the truth, and the life." He does not say: "I give to you
the way and the truth and the life," as if he effected
all this in me from without. It is within me that he
must stay, live, speak . . . so that we are righteous in
God's sight in him. . . .[195]

Obviously we are hearing two men, each with his own
style of thinking. The interplay of their similarities and their
differences provided the foundation for Lutheran theology
and continues to be the topic of much discussion.

Melanchthon never claimed to be a carbon copy of Luther. His talents complemented rather than duplicated
Luther's. As teacher, spokesman, and diplomat of the
Reformation, his "mature" theology takes on a cast of its
own, one which determined, in many ways, the course of
later Lutheran theology. To this topic we now turn.

CHAPTER THREE

Theologian

Scholars are fond of speaking about the "young" Luther or the "mature" Luther. If we borrow these terms for Melanchthon, we would have to say that the "mature" Melanchthon emerged in the half-decade between 1530 and 1535, from the writing of the *Augsburg Confession* to the new *Loci* edition of 1535.

In the *Augsburg Confession,* Melanchthon formulated a statement of belief for the evangelical church and also for his own theology. After a decade of probing and developing, he now declared—on behalf of the church and himself—"This is where we stand." In the *Apology,* or defense, of the *Confession* he worked out the doctrine of justification in greater detail. This was the first manifesto of his "mature" thought on this central doctrine, and it was followed a year later by an even longer exposition in the *Romans Commentary* of 1532.

With the appearance of the second *Loci* edition of 1535, it became apparent that Melanchthon's thought had undergone significant development from the first *Loci* of 1521. With this edition Melanchthon came to terms with the "widening front," the challenge of the radical Reformation on the left. This new *Loci* set the tone for all succeeding editions.

The New *Loci* Editions

During the 1520's the Wittenberg Reformers must have wondered if the Reformation was not getting out of hand. The Swiss Reformation, first under Zwingli, later under Calvin, opened up many areas of doctrinal discussion. The South German evangelicals around Martin Bucer often formed a mediating group between Saxony and Switzerland, but the most vexing concern came from the Baptists and Enthusiasts who swarmed all over northern Europe. The Wittenberg theologians had retained those Roman Catholic traditions which they believed were not expressly rejected by the Scriptures. The Baptists and Enthusiasts, on the other hand, tended to sweep all traditions away.

The sharpest debate with the radical movements involved Christology. The spark which set off the battle was Karlstadt's and Zwingli's disagreement with Luther on the Lord's Supper. It is interesting to note how differently Luther and Melanchthon reacted to this, because their reactions pinpointed a significant contrast in their outlooks.

Luther and the Christological Controversy

The heart of Luther's Christology was the overwhelming truth of the incarnation: in Jesus Christ *God had become man.* For Luther, the question of accepting the Christology of the ancient church was no issue; the ancient Christological formulas lay at the heart of his faith. Repeatedly he emphasized Christ's divinity and his humanity. But above all, Christ's two natures could not be considered separately, for to Luther the great truth was that God had fully united himself with man in Jesus Christ. God revealed himself in Christ's humanity. Luther wrote:

> When we say, "Christ, the man, is creator of heaven and earth, in whom we believe and trust, and to whom we should pray," we are not speaking just about a man apart from God. We refer to the man or person who is both God and man, in one undivided and unseparated person—God incarnated. We speak about him, not in abstract terms, as the ancients put it, but in concrete: Christ, God's and Mary's son, is creator of the heavens and the earth . . . and is in his divinity and humanity one single undivided person.[196]

It is not difficult to see how Luther's concept of the uniting of the finite and infinite in Christ—*finitum capax infiniti est*—and the *communicatio idiomatum*[197] played such a strong role in his faith. Luther's Christology was thoroughly incarnational, the dogma of the ancient church as its assumed foundation.

Luther's violent reaction to Karlstadt and Zwingli can be understood only when one realizes this. The merest suggestion that in the Eucharist Christ's human nature was not fully present meant for Luther that the ancient doctrine of the eternal union of the two natures was compromised. He considered all talk of Christ's mere "spiritual presence" in the Sacrament an outgrowth of ancient heresies. From his pulpit he charged:

I have seen and noticed that the devil wishes to
revive these old heresies through the new sects and
sacramentarians, who divide and split the person of
Christ.[198]

In his thunderous rejection of Karlstadt, "Against the
Heavenly Prophets," Luther insisted that to deny Christ's
bodily presence was to deny the total union of God and
man in Christ—and that contradicted what for Luther was
the very center of the Christian faith:

> . . . they finally come to the point where they will deny
> that Christ is God. For to reason it sounds just as foolish
> to say, "Man is God," as, "The bread is the body." And
> as they deny the one they will soon also boldly deny the
> other. Such is also the aim of the devil, who has led
> them away from Scripture into their own reason, thereby
> bringing back again all the ancient heresies.[199]

In 1527 Luther wrote his article "That These Words of
Christ 'This Is My Body' Still Stand Firm," not only against
Karlstadt, but also against Zwingli and John Oecolampadius,
and all others who rejected Christ's bodily presence in the
Sacrament. When the Swiss looked to John 6:63 for support
(". . . the flesh is of no avail"), Luther retorted that one
cannot accept just part of Christ, and he listed the heresies
which rejected Christ's true humanity.[200] When they said
that a body cannot be in many places simultaneously but is
confined to God's right hand, Luther replied that God's
right hand is everywhere:

> Christ's body is at the right hand of God; that is granted.
> The right hand of God, however, is everywhere. . . .

Therefore it surely is present also in the bread and wine at table. Now where the right hand of God is, there Christ's body and blood must be. . . .[201]

In his next contribution to the Lord's Supper discussion, the *Great Confession* of 1528, Luther summarized his fundamental concern:

My grounds on which I rest in this matter are as follows: The first is this article of our faith, that Jesus Christ is essential, natural, true, complete God and man in one person, undivided and inseparable.[202]

Luther's Christology, thus far developed in the Lord's Supper controversies, had brought him to these convictions:

1. The central truth of Jesus Christ is that God has united himself with man, a union of two natures so complete and intertwined that they can never again be thought of separately. One nature cannot be present in the Lord's Supper without the other.

2. Since Christ's body is at the right hand of God, which is everywhere, and since it is forever united with the divine nature, the Logos, which is wherever God is, it follows that Christ is everywhere *(ubique)*—the "ubiquity" of Christ's body.

3. This is possible only because, in uniting with the divine nature, the human nature shares *(communicatio)* the characteristics *(idiomatum)* of the divine nature in the person of Jesus Christ.[203]

The Christology of the ancient church was soon be-

leaguered from other quarters. In their zeal to purify the
church of false doctrine, some Enthusiasts looked upon the
Trinity itself as a scripturally unwarranted teaching. Anticipating the Unitarians of later centuries, they disavowed
Christ's divinity.

Luther took relatively little notice of these radicals. Since
Karlstadt and the Swiss had already undermined the orthodox doctrine of Christ, as he saw it, these left-wing aberra-
tions were just outgrowths of the same tendency. In a letter
of February 1525 to Johannes Briesmann in Königsberg,
Luther reports how a former schoolmaster of Nürnberg had
become anti-Trinitarian "in the spirit of Karlstadt." [204] Luther had exerted his energy in his battles over the Lord's
Supper. Any new attacks on Christ were just variations of
Karlstadt's and the Sacramentarians' deviations.

Melanchthon and the Christological Debates

Melanchthon's reaction to these issues was significantly
different. The reason for this difference is basic: His overarching concern was the justifying *beneficium Christi*, the
redemptive work of Christ. We have already noted that
Melanchthon emphasized above all what Christ had done to
save us. Luther's great emphasis was *the person of Christ
himself*, the union of God and man in the incarnation.
Melanchthon concentrated primarily on *Christ's redemptive
work*, particularly the cross. Obviously the incarnation was
part of his faith, but it was a secondary motif to the Lord's
redemptive acts.

Even in his early works Melanchthon's thought was incarnational so as to affirm the saving *beneficia Christi*. In

the Humanist-colored Matthew lectures the emphasis on the incarnation stressed Christ's ability to resist the devil and obey the Law. In the *Annotations to John* the incarnation, particularly Christ's divinity, was accented, but primarily as a guarantee of Christ's work.[205] Melanchthon did not dwell on the incarnation as deeply as did Luther, but spent his efforts affirming the truth of justification.

This concern also suggests why Melanchthon reacted differently to the question of the Lord's Supper. This controversy did not menace the heart of his Christology, as was the case with Luther. Karlstadt, Zwingli, and the others did not take direct issue with Christ's saving work, which was Melanchthon's chief consideration. For Luther the Sacramentarians were a threat to his very faith; for Melanchthon the question was a tragic case of the evangelical cause splintering over a theological issue.

He did, however, express himself on the problem, and his opinions strongly supported Luther. In 1525 he penned a statement about Karlstadt. "Surely there is no reason to divide Christ and to say that he is present with us according to his divinity but not present according to his humanity," he wrote.[206] He referred to 1 Corinthians 10:16 ("The bread . . . is it not a participation in the body of Christ?") and agreed with Luther that Karlstadt and his friends had followed their reason instead of the Scriptures. He did not charge, however, that they jeopardized the incarnation itself, as Luther insisted.

Melanchthon wrote two interesting letters to his friend Balthasar Thuring in Coburg in 1527 and 1528. On November 18, 1527, he expressed his feeling that the correct under-

standing of the Lord's Supper must be held without compromise, although the laity in the congregations might not
understand the complicated issues: "It is enough . . . if the
people know that the body of Christ is present in the
Eucharist, according to the divine promise and ordination." [207] He added that this was the teaching of the ancient
church, but he did not connect the Sacramentarians with the
ancient Christological heresies.

In the second letter, written early in 1528, Melanchthon
affirmed his agreement with Luther concerning the ubiquity
of Christ: "Christ is exalted above all creatures and is everywhere present." [208] Note particularly that Melanchthon assumed the ubiquitous presence of Christ's *person,* not just
specifically one nature or the other. This seemingly small
distinction played a great part in later discussions.

On April 8, 1529, Melanchthon wrote his well-known open
letter to John Oecolampadius, in which he defended Luther's teachings. He pointed to Matthew 20:28, "where there
is no basis to split the divinity from the humanity; from
this I am convinced that the Sacrament is the testimony of
his true presence." [209] He again mentioned 1 Corinthians
10:16, which later became a favorite verse in terms of the
Eucharist.

During the Marburg Colloquy with the Swiss in 1529,
Zwingli reassured him that he held firmly to the doctrine
of the two natures and Christ's divinity. Melanchthon noted
with satisfaction that Zwingli did not sympathize with the
anti-Trinitarians. Until that time, Melanchthon had been
confident that the Wittenberg view of the Lord's Supper

represented the teachings of the ancient church.[210] He was, therefore, shaken in the summer of 1530 when Oecolampadius answered with his *Dialogus*, a collection of ancient texts which lent support to the Swiss viewpoint. Even so, Melanchthon continued to defend Luther on the basis of the Scriptures.[211]

Article 10 of the *Augsburg Confession* sums up very briefly what Luther and Melanchthon believed without going into any of the related questions:

> . . . the body and blood of Christ are truly present and are distributed to those who eat in the Supper of the Lord. . . .[212]

During that summer, however, Melanchthon began to deal with some of these related issues, suggesting the direction his thoughts were to go later. First, he says that though Christ's body was real, the fact that he was also divine meant that he could be everywhere.[213] Nor can we divide Christ, as Nestorius did, but must insist that *the whole Christ* is present.[214]

Secondly, in his "Judgment Concerning Zwingli's Doctrine" he hesitated to use Luther's term "bodily ubiquity of Christ," that is, the ubiquity of Christ's human nature. He affirmed, rather, the ubiquity of *Christ's whole person:* "Christ the person, or the whole Christ, is present among all creatures."[215] This included, of course, both natures, but Melanchthon preferred not to speak of them separately. Like Luther he had to define clearly what he meant in terms of the *communicatio idiomatum,* which he later did.

Thirdly, in this "Judgment" he again gave us an insight into his future thought by excluding not only transubstantiation but also rejecting any idea of locating or limiting Christ's body strictly within the bread.[216] He feared, perhaps more than Luther, the almost superstitious piety of the Middle Ages, where the bread was venerated as being or containing Christ's body. True, Melanchthon still used the term "in bread and wine," but in the coming years the preposition "with" increasingly replaced "in." Indeed, in this "Judgment" he also wrote that "we place the true and real presence of Christ's body *with* the bread." [217]

Actually, Melanchthon was particularly disturbed by the bitterness caused by the problem of the Lord's Supper. In his letter to Oecolampadius he expressed with deep feeling his hope that their disagreement would not disrupt their long-standing friendship.[218] Melanchthon suspected that much of the controversy concerned a fundamental misunderstanding about vocabulary.[219] For his part, he would have preferred to emphasize the Sacrament's use and purpose within the church and not become so involved in the theological disputes. Dr. Peter Fraenkel is quite right in concluding that Melanchthon's main interest in the Sacrament was "functional" rather than theological.[220]

What he always hoped for was that the evangelicals could achieve harmony by agreeing on a simple, clear formulation of basic belief. As late as 1534 he wrote:

> It should be confessed that in the giving of the elements, bread and wine, Christ is truly and substantially present. Indeed, I would require no more than that. . . .[221]

How different from Luther, who was convinced that the difference in theological details represented an irreconcilable chasm and even a dire threat to the Christian faith!

Where Luther had considered Karlstadt and the Zwinglians a danger to the Christian faith, with the anti-Trinitarians merely their logical outgrowth, Melanchthon's reaction was the opposite. He disagreed with Karlstadt and Zwingli, but never thought them a menace to the faith. In the Baptist anti-Trinitarians, however, he saw a rejection of the central truth of Christianity: the benefits of Christ, his redemptive work. We have seen how Melanchthon avoided Trinitarian and Christological dogma in the first *Loci*, but when dealing with the Gospel of John in 1523 he had emphasized most strongly the divinity of Christ; the *beneficia Christi* were valid only because Christ was God. Karlstadt and Zwingli never denied the fact, but the anti-Trinitarians did.

Near the end of the 1520's, Melanchthon took note of the growing anti-Trinitarian tendencies in Baptist circles.[222] In 1529 he wrote his friend Joachim Camerarius that what the church needed was a "handbook of Christian doctrine," outlining the dogmas of the church, especially concerning Christ's divinity.[223] In 1530 he had to deal personally with Campanus, an anti-Trinitarian who denied Christ's divinity, and he became firmly convinced of the danger this threat represented.

In Melanchthon's opinion, however, the real danger came from the Spaniard Michael Servetus, who argued with deep conviction and sharp intelligence that the doctrine of the

Trinity and Christ's divinity were not scriptural. Very likely Servetus appeared in Augsburg when Melanchthon was writing the *Confession,* and if so, he was doubtless a thorn in the side during the discussions. Articles 1 and 3 of the *Confession* make it quite clear that the Wittenberg Reformers rejected these radical tendencies and held to the ancient doctrines of God and Christ.[224]

Melanchthon had shown growing concern over the radicals among the German Enthusiasts, but with the appearance of Servetus this concern turned into alarm. "Good Lord!" he exclaimed in a letter to his closest friend, Camerarius, "what calamities might erupt if these inquiries continue further, whether the Logos or the Spirit really are persons!" [225] Servetus had struck the central nerve in Melanchthon's faith by striking at Christ's divinity—which was never attacked in the Sacramentarian disputes—and it was inevitable that Melanchthon would be compelled to marshal his powers in defense. He gave a hint about his future plans when he wrote Johannes Brenz in the summer of 1533:

> I read the *Loci Communes* over again and am about to prepare a new edition with some changes, in which I shall deal with these matters.[226]

The Trinity

In the first *Loci* Melanchthon condemned all speculation about God and Christ and did not deal with the ancient orthodox doctrines. He wished only to exalt the saving work of Christ. Ten years later, however, he had discovered that these *beneficia* were being undermined by those who denied the ancient traditions.

Melanchthon found it necessary, therefore, to begin his second *Loci* edition with a thorough review of Trinitarian and Christological dogma, not because he suddenly had become fond of such speculation, but because he was defending the truth of Christ's saving work. Scholars may argue that Melanchthon went into unnecessarily complex detail in later *Loci* editions, but there can be no doubt that his motive for doing so was to protect the central Reformation teaching of salvation and justification.

One of the opening paragraphs of the second *Loci* edition (1535) set the theme. Melanchthon pointed to John 14, "the admonition of Christ, when Philip asked him the greatest and most significant of all questions, that is, the question concerning the nature of God: 'Lord, show us the Father. . . .'"[227] Christ's answer was the cornerstone of Melanchthon's theology. "He who has seen me has seen the Father. . . ."

Melanchthon was not interested in pondering the mysterious nature of God. For him, "to know God" was to know his will for men, his anger against sin, the sending of his Son, and the Gospel of his grace. Since the Father revealed himself through the Son, we know him only through Christ, and we can be certain of this *only because* Christ is truly God himself.[228] His divinity was the guarantee for his work, his mission, and his message, Melanchthon believed. A mere man could not have sacrificed himself for us, risen from the dead, sit at God's right hand, and be eternally present among believers. Undermine this pillar of Christ's divinity and the whole body of faith collapses. Now that this had been challenged, Melanchthon had to go back and deal with the dogma of the ancient church, not to speculate but to affirm the faith in God's redemptive work.

Melanchthon had no intention of expanding the ancient dogmas, or developing them further. He occupied himself with these questions for the next 30 years, but contributed nothing particularly original from his own thought. He saw his task as one of explanation, clarification, and defense.

He began with the objection of the anti-Trinitarians, that the Trinity meant tri-theism, three Gods. In the section "That God is One" he said that there was one divine substance *(substantia* or *ousia)*. Furthermore, borrowing from Augustine and the Scholastics, he maintained that one could not distinguish between the substance of God and his attributes.[229] God's substance and attributes are identical.

This sounds technical, but, in fact, this point became crucial. This meant that the Son, sharing the divine substance, also shared the divine attributes. Consequently, the Son can be everywhere present, because ubiquity is an attribute of the Father and, therefore, a support for the "Lutheran" doctrine of the Lord's Supper.

Melanchthon spent an enormous amount of time and effort establishing that the Father, Son, and Holy Spirit are each a person *(persona)* within the Trinity, sharing the same substance *(homoousia)*. He insisted that each person is separate from the other but more than just three differing appearances, or one actor playing three roles, or three dif-

fering areas of work.[230] In later works he spoke of two ways
to distinguish the three persons:

> One is inward, that is, the Father begetting, the Son
> begotten, and the Spirit proceeding. The other is out-
> ward, derived from their benefits toward the church.[231]

In distinguishing the persons inwardly he used the same
metaphors which he mentioned in his *Annotations to John*
in 1523: "The Father, considering himself, begets a certain
thought, which is his image." [232] Though this is similar to
the human thought process, there is a decisive difference:
"We do not transfer our essence into this image." [233] So the
Son or Logos is the "word" or "image" of the Father—something other than the Father, a person in his own right, but
begotten from and sharing fully the divine substance. The
Spirit is the force *(agitator, agitatio)* or moving power *(vis
agens)*, which proceeds from the Father and the Son, also a
person of the one divine substance.[234]

Melanchthon had much more to say about the "outward"
distinctions of the three persons. The second person of the
Trinity, the Son, "took human nature upon himself from the
Virgin Mary at a certain time . . . neither the Father nor the
Holy Spirit took human nature upon themselves." [235] The
work of the Son was defined broadly to encompass the total
mediation between God and man, from speaking to the Old
Testament prophets, through the incarnation, and up to the
present time, when he eternally intercedes for the church.[236]

As have ancient and modern theologians in general, Melanchthon had difficulty defining clearly the distinctive work

of the Spirit. He did mention the appearance of the Spirit as a dove during Jesus' baptism.[237] Ultimately, he concluded, God's activity could never be divided neatly into the works of each person. He used the Augustinian formula: "The works of the Trinity beyond itself are indivisible," [238] which simply meant that, in the work of the Son, the Father and the Spirit are also present, and vice versa.

All in all, today's reader might be grateful for Melanchthon's outline of the ancient dogma, but he will hardly be inspired by it. One senses, upon reading his works, that the review of Trinitarian doctrine was for Melanchthon always a *prolegomena,* a foundation for the doctrine of the redemption through the Logos, the Son.

It was the doctrine of the Logos which claimed Melanchthon's urgent attention. His task was twofold: to show that the Logos was divine, and to show that the Logos, the Son, was a person. On the first he spent little time, stating that John 1:1 leaves no doubt that, "In the beginning was the Word . . . and the Word was God." With that, he dismissed Arius and those who followed him.[239]

The second opinion, that the Logos was not a separate person from the Father, was the critical matter, since Servetus argued that there could be only one indivisible God. Melanchthon felt that if the Logos were not a person, then Jesus Christ finally was not truly God. He returned to the Gospel of John and proposed that the phrase "and the Word was with God" indicated that the Word was distinct from the Father. He also referred to John 1:14 ("And the Word became flesh . . .") and argued:

Now the Father did not put on human nature, and he distinguished himself from the Son, saying, "This is my Son." Finally, when it is written "The Word became flesh," one must understand it as a person. . . . Therefore the Logos is a person. Furthermore, if the Logos were only the thinking of the Father himself, this thinking would not have become flesh.[240]

In presenting his argument, Melanchthon cited not only countless Scripture passages, but reviewed the discussions of the early church as well. Convinced that Servetus' arguments were no more than a repetition of ancient heresy, particularly that of Paul of Samosata,[241] Melanchthon confidently concluded that the Wittenberg Reformers were faithful to both Scriptures and the early church. This "return to tradition," which many feel was a concession Melanchthon made to Rome, really reflected the feeling of the Reformers that the evangelical cause was not only scriptural, but directly in line with the ancient church. The Bible was unquestionably the norm for doctrine, but ever since the Diet of Augsburg this bond with the ancient church was a key affirmation of the Reformation.

Once Melanchthon had reintroduced Trinitarian and Christological doctrine into his later *Loci* editions, he set the precedent for his students, who became the next generation of Lutheran teachers. They went into the matter in even greater detail, producing ultimately the enormously exhaustive treatments of the "orthodox Lutheran fathers" of the next century. Often, however, their work became fully as speculative as that of the Scholastics which the Reformers had so disliked.

Jesus Christ—God and Man

In examining Melanchthon's mature teaching about the incarnation, one realizes how closely he allied himself with the "Alexandrian" school. First, he began his Christology, as did Athanasius and Cyril, with the Logos.[242] Second, he read church history from the Alexandrian viewpoint, condemning all that was anti-Alexandrian heresies.[243] Third, he spoke always of Christ's person and work in terms of the whole person, the total union of the two natures. Fourth, he used the phrases of Cyril, the "concrete" person and the "abstract" natures, to explain this union.

The foundation of Melanchthon's Christology was the Logos. Having demonstrated that the Logos, God's Son, was both divine and a person, he now proceeded to the doctrine of the incarnation. His oft-repeated formula was: "It is correctly and usually stated thus: The person of the Logos assumes *(assumpsit)* human nature." [244] It is a complete "hypostatic" union, one *hyphistamenon,* as he often wrote.

Melanchthon's constant emphasis was on the inseparability of the two natures, not unlike Luther's concern. Not only was this union complete in Jesus Christ, but it remained so in eternity.[245] He compared it to the union of mind (or spirit) and body in a human being—neither can exist without the other. In the examination he wrote for ordination candidates Melanchthon defined this unique presence of God's logos on earth by describing four "modes" of God's presence: [246]

1. The first is a universal presence, wherein for the preservation of all things God is present with all

creatures. But though present, God is still something other than, apart from, or separate from these. . . .

2. The second is God's presence with angels and men in heaven. . . .

3. The third presence is within the lives of the regenerated. . . . Here, too, God is present apart from or separate from them. . . .

4. The fourth is quite different, in which the person of the Logos assumes human nature, not only inseparately . . . but is one *hyphistamenon.*

It is no wonder that the Logos became the dominating force in the incarnation. We are not speaking of a man, Jesus of Nazareth, to whom God came and united himself, but of the Son, the Logos, who assumed human nature. Melanchthon, of course, affirmed the full humanity of Jesus, but the Logos is obviously the dynamic agent in the person of Christ.[247]

Now that Melanchthon had affirmed the total and complete union of the two natures—divine and human—in the person of Jesus Christ, it became necessary to clarify how they relate or work together. This sounds technical, but it is a basic theological question, current even today in ecumenical discussions. Melanchthon contributed not only insight to the matter, but, above all, a good dose of common sense.

We are dealing with the formidable term, the *communicatio idiomatum,* the "exchange of properties" or the "sharing of characteristics." To put it simply: How do the two differing natures fit together into one person?

Melanchthon borrowed two helpful terms from Cyril of Alexandria—"abstract" and "concrete." We can speak of each nature in Christ, Melanchthon said, but we are doing so "in the abstract," since the nature no longer exists by itself, but is part of the one, united person.

> A proposition in the abstract refers to a nature considered by itself. One would have to say, for example, "the divine nature does not die." [248]

Speaking in the abstract, we retain the specific properties of each nature: the divine nature is all-knowing, invulnerable, while the human nature hungers, suffers, and dies.

When we speak "concretely," we speak of the whole person of Christ, and the concrete person embraces both natures. *The properties of both natures are shared by or communicated to the concrete person.* Melanchthon wrote:

> This way of speaking "in the concrete" the Fathers of the Church call the *communicatio idiomatum,* a form of speech in which the properties of the natures are rightly attributed to the person.[249]

We do this on a human level when we say, "The man counts," never saying only, "The mind counts," even though that is actually the case.[250]

Abstractly, it is true that "the divine nature does not die," but in the personal union we say concretely, "Christ died," because the human nature which died was a part of the person. In the concrete sense we can even say that "God died," because the person on the cross was truly God.[251]

Furthermore, Christ's work always involved his person: Mediator, Redeemer, Savior, King, Priest, Shepherd—all these refer to the works and are the titles of the concrete person. He was not mediator according to one or the other abstract nature, but as a concrete, whole person.[252] Christ's mission was as one God-man person, not one nature or another alternately acting by itself.

This rule of *communicatio idiomatum* gives us a glimpse into the fact that God united himself fully with men in Jesus Christ. Melanchthon declared:

> We retain the difference in the natures, but at the same time . . . because of the personal union these statements are true: God suffered, was crucified, and died. Do not think that human nature alone, not the whole Son of God, was Redeemer! For even if the divine nature was not wounded and did not die, nonetheless you know that this Son, coeternal with the Father, is the Redeemer. For that account these precepts have been handed down in the doctrine of the *communicatio idiomatum.*[253]

Melanchthon was convinced that whatever Christ does, from the incarnation to the present, is an action of the total person. To speak "abstractly" about each nature separately is to speculate, he believed. The proclamation must always be what Christ, the God-man person, is and does.

The *communicatio idiomatum* played a dominant role in later Lutheran theology. The *Formula of Concord* took great pains to clarify it,[254] but it also took into consideration Luther's outlook, which was distinctive from Melanchthon's and received vastly detailed treatment by Lutheran theologians of the 1600's. Martin Chemnitz, a student of both Luther and Melanchthon, sketched three kinds *(genera)* of *communicatio,* which the next generation of Lutheran theologians labeled thus: [255]

1. *Genus idiomaticum,* where the characteristics *(idiomata)* of each nature are ascribed to the person.

2. *Genus apotelesmaticum,* where the works of Christ *(apotelesmata),* whether of one nature or both, are ascribed to the person.

3. *Genus majestaticum,* where the human nature receives and shares the "majestic" attributes of the divine nature.

The first two types of *communicatio* were articulated by Melanchthon, but he stopped short of the third *genus.* He felt that one should speak concretely about the whole person and not abstractly about the natures, which are present in the person anyway. The *communicatio* was best understood as the sharing within the person, not one nature abstractly with another.

The third *genus,* however, summarized Luther's concern in the battle over the Lord's Supper: The human nature shares the attributes of the divine nature, and can therefore be ubiquitous. Now we can see the difference in outlook between the two men developing into a rather clear difference of expression. Luther affirmed the exchange of natures with each other in order to establish his conviction regarding Christ's physical presence in the Lord's Supper; Melanchthon emphasized the union of natures into the whole person of Christ to guard against speculation while maintaining Christ's presence.

God's Wrath—Man's Sin

Following our discussion on the incarnation, the next topic should deal with the saving work of Christ. We must pause, however, and examine how Melanchthon finally portrayed the doctrine of sin, which in turn largely dictated how he understood the work of Christ.

This is an area where Melanchthon had made a good deal of adjustment from Humanism, breaking sharply from the Humanist view in the *Loci* and the *Annotations on John,* for example. At Augsburg in 1530 it was necessary to summarize the Reformation doctrine of sin. In doing so, he pulled together his own conclusions, setting the course of his later theology as well:

> Our churches also teach that since the fall of Adam all men who are propagated according to nature are born in sin. That is to say, they are without fear of God, are without trust in God, and are concupiscent. And this disease or vice of origin is truly sin, which even now damns and brings eternal death. . . .[256]

Luther realized not only from Scriptures, but, above all, from his own spiritual struggles, that sin is primarily a broken relationship with God. This insight became the cornerstone of the evangelical doctrine of sin. Melanchthon summed it up in the *Confession,* but was called upon to defend the teaching in the *Apology*. After the *Confession* was read, Roman theologians prepared a *Confutation*, sharply criticizing this second article. Article 2 of the *Apology* was as thorough a review of Melanchthon's teaching on sin as anything he wrote in later years.

Melanchthon asserted that the Scholastics misunderstood the ancient church and therefore minimized original sin. "They argue that the inclination to evil is a quality of the body." [257] Then he charged:

> By such questions they miss the main issue. Thus when they talk about original sin, they do not mention the more serious faults of human nature, namely, ignoring God, despising him, lacking fear and trust in him, hating his judgment and fleeing it, being angry at him, despairing of his grace, trusting in temporal things.[258]

In other words, the Reformation shifted the center of sin from the body to the spirit. Sin is a spiritual lack, a separation from God, which then filters through everything man is and does.

Melanchthon went back to the old Augustinian-Scholastic formula: "Original sin is the lack of original righteousness." He then asked, "But what is righteousness?" [259] For his answer he turned to Scripture: Righteousness is not just the second table of the Ten Commandments, "but also the first, commanding fear of God, faith and love toward him." [260] When man was created in God's image and likeness, surely this was his righteousness.[261]

In the fall of Adam and Eve man lost his intimate knowledge, trust, and love of God. Having lost the ability to obey the first table of the law, he slid into concupiscence, "not merely a corruption of the physical constitution, but the evil inclination of man's higher capacities toward carnal things." [262] The spiritual pride which caused the first sin spread its infection to the whole man, spirit and body, and man was trapped into disobedience of the whole law.

Thus the evangelical definition of sin always includes these two elements: "lack of ability to trust, fear, or love God; and concupiscence, which pursues carnal ends contrary to the Word of God." [263]

Melanchthon went farther by insisting that there was no way man could bring about a relationship to God by himself: ". . . we deny the existence not only of actual fear and trust in God but also the possibility and gift to produce it." [264] Since he believed this was true of every human born according to nature, it followed that this was a sin of our very origin, or "original sin." It was not mere guilt, as the *Confutation* argued, but sin, because sin was this spiritual "disease" into which all are born.

Since his first years as a Reformer Melanchthon always regarded natural man as capable of knowing something about God through his reason, simply because it was obvious that many people believed in God without the Christian Gospel. In the *Annotations to John* of 1523 Melanchthon conceded that natural man knew God existed, and even that he was a just God. He carried this line of thought even farther in his later years and outlined all the traditional, rational "proofs" of God's existence as philosophers and theologians over the years had formulated them. In the last

Loci edition he listed nine "proofs" of God's existence, gleaned from his studies.[265]

His purpose in doing so, however, was quite different from that of the Scholastics, who regarded man's natural knowledge of God as the "first step" toward revelation. Melanchthon's whole point, from his *Annotations* onward, was that any and all of natural's man's notions of God led him inevitably away from true faith in God. God could not be truly known, believed, and trusted in, apart from the Gospel in Christ. His goal was to exalt revelation as our only source of full knowledge of God. The Lutheran theologians of the next century, however, devoted a great deal more effort toward substantiating these "proofs," so that the matter became almost an independent section of theology. Luther was not one whit concerned with "proofs" of God's existence, being in that respect more in tune with the twentieth century than either Melanchthon or the seventeenth century Lutheran theologians.

Melanchthon summed up his convictions concerning the depth of sin in the 1535 *Loci* by speaking again of both "original sin" and "actual sin." Original sin is that condition described in the *Augsburg Confession,* and this results in actual sins. Melanchthon could not emphasize the extent of sin strongly enough; man is caught in a downward spiral, unable to extricate himself. Because he cannot obey God, he inevitably disobeys both tables of the Law; his disobedience, in turn, drives him even farther away from God. If natural man tries to please God with works, he ends up in self-righteous Phariseeism, but if he realizes his disability to obey the Law, he is plunged into a despair where he can only hate God as a judge.

Both as a Humanist and Reformer, Melanchthon was concerned with the issue of the freedom of the will. Luther had praised his *Annotations to John* commentary of 1523 because Melanchthon, in depicting this downward spiral, had strongly excluded man's will in the matter of salvation. On the other hand, he shared with the Humanists a deep suspicion of any sort of determinism which would undermine man's ethical responsibility.[266]

The noisy blow-up between Luther and Erasmus over this very issue in the mid-1520's shook Melanchthon deeply. Luther asserted the bondage of the will, and Erasmus its freedom. Melanchthon's position—supporting Luther, with one extra comment—was summed up in Article 18 of the *Confession*. It was the position taken in the first *Loci* of 1521 and to which he adhered the remainder of his life. He began with the extra comment:

> Our churches teach that man's will has some liberty for
> the attainment of civil righteousness and for the choice
> of things subject to reason.[267]

This statement secured the will's ability and responsibility against determinism, but such freedom, however, had nothing to do with man's religious capacity, for he then continued with the heart of the matter:

> However, it does not have the power, without the Holy
> Spirit, to attain the righteousness of God—that is,
> spiritual righteousness—because natural man does not

perceive the gifts of the Spirit of God; but this righteousness is wrought in the heart when the Holy Spirit
is received through the Word.[268]

Against God, man's will is helpless to obey, trust, love, or
believe in him. Righteousness is not something man wills or
attains; it comes to him from outside, through God's Word,
and is effected from outside, by God's Spirit coming to him.
Melanchthon never wavered from this affirmation: in matters of faith and righteousness, man's will was not free, but
enslaved.[269]

If natural man inescapably disobeys the Law, of what
purpose, then, is the Law? The first use of the Law is a universal one—civil, political, or pedagogical—the need for all
societies to be governed by laws in order that peace and
order might be maintained. Without law there would be only
chaos and anarchy.[270]

"The second and proper office of the divine Law is the
principal one, namely to show sin, to accuse, terrify, and
condemn consciences." [271] This use of the Law Melanchthon
had, of course, always taught, together with Paul and
Luther. We hear the Law and realize our sin.[272]

Having heard the Law and acknowledged our sin, we are
confronted by the withering judgment of God's wrath. "No
creature could sustain the wrath of God; 'God is a consuming fire.'" [273] From this there is no escape, "for man knows
that God is angry over against sin, and that he will not set
aside his wrath." [274]

There is no earthly way that we can satisfy God's anger
over our sin.[275] The sinner under the Law is tormented by

the knowledge that God is just and that his anger is un-remitting against our sin. The Law brings us to this point and opens the way for the Gospel.

The Redemptive Work of Christ

Thus the Law sets the stage for the Gospel, which is, above all, the proclamation of the "benefits" of Christ.

> In Romans 1:17 Paul adds the sum of the Gospel, the presentation of the whole argument, when he says, "For in it the righteousness of God is revealed through faith." This is the sum of all Christ's benefits.[276]

In view of the preceding section, it is clear what Christ's mission must be:

1. To reveal God as he is, setting right all the false ideas of man.

2. To suffer the consequences of man's sin and placate God's wrath.

3. To continue his work as God-man mediator through all time.

The broad context of Christ's mission is as "mediator." The Son's mediating work embraces all he does as Logos, from the creation and the incarnation and continuing on through his presence in the church and believers today. In all things God mediates himself to the world through his Word, the Son. Consider this sweeping synopsis of his mission:

The eternal Son is the second person of the divinity . . . through whom the Father spoke the decree and whole order of the creation and man's renewal; and the Son was sent that he might directly reveal the Gospel; he assumed human nature, is Mediator, Redeemer, and Savior, gathering the church as a human family by the voice of the Gospel and restoring it to eternal life.[277]

The purpose of the Son's mission as mediator is increasingly described by Melanchthon with the words *communicatio-communicare,* a communication, sharing, or participation. He wrote that the final reason for the creation was that

God wishes that creatures might share *(communicet)* his goodness, and indeed communicates *(communicat)* with rational creatures those things which are most sublime in him, namely wisdom, righteousness, freedom of choice, eternal life.[278]

This sharing between God and man was lost in the fall of Adam and Eve, but God communicated himself to man through the Son, finally uniting the Son with human nature in full sharing or communion. [279] The incarnated Christ became a pattern for the restoration of God's sharing himself with man once again.

Christ, therefore, affirms that the race of man was created for this purpose, that God might share his abundant goodness, which is most profoundly illustrated in the union of the divine and human natures in the Son. Thus Paul says that "in the Son all things were created" (Col. 1:16), so that this marvelous work of God might be made clear, in which he shared with human nature his goodness, that even in a personal union the Son assumed human nature.[280]

The broad context of the Son's work as mediator was to be the restoring agent of God's communion with man, the most perfect example of which was the personal union of the two natures in Christ. From here we examine specific aspects of Christ's saving mission.

Christ the Revealer

Considering what Melanchthon taught about the Trinity and about man's deficient knowledge of God and his fear of the Law, it is obvious that he believed that one of Christ's tasks was to reveal the Gospel, the message of a loving God. Christ's reply to Philip is one of the basic passages in Scripture: "He who has seen me has seen the Father." [281] Melanchthon reminded his readers of the scriptural terms— the Son as Word (in the Gospel of John) and image of the invisible God (Hebrews 1:15), both of which focus on Christ as revealer.

The principal thrust of the Gospel centers on the saving acts of Christ—the cross and the resurrection. The cross, above all, reveals God, for it shows the depth of his love in his willingness to send his Son to suffer for us.

Melanchthon's emphasis on Christ as revealer of the Father was the same as Luther's term "theology of the Cross," which asserted that God is known, not through philosophical or theological speculation *(theologia gloriae)*, but through the cross of Christ. This thoroughly Christological knowledge of God has been a hallmark of Lutheran theology ever since.

Christ the Sacrifice

Disobedient man stands under the curse of God's judgment.

> In this torment the Gospel puts forth for us the mediator, Jesus Christ, God's only begotten Son, who became man, and testifies that the mediator Christ fulfilled the ransom and satisfaction for all our sins and gained for us grace.[282]

When Melanchthon wrote specifically about Christ's justifying work, his thoughts were centered on the cross. This meant that the first *Loci* of 1521 set the tone for his later theology. The Humanist emphasis of the early Matthew lectures—Christ as victor over Satan in resisting the temptation to disobey—and of the dominant themes of the *Annotations to John* lectures of 1523—Christ as the example of human life—fade into second place. The cross stands supreme as the overarching *beneficium Christi*. Though Luther used more varied and descriptive language to portray Christ's work, surely he, too, viewed the sacrifice on the cross as the climax of his mission.

Like Luther, Melanchthon never systematically presented a doctrine of Christ's sacrifice. The teaching doesn't stand by itself but colors every part of his theology. Moreover, he used the various scriptural and doctrinal terms almost interchangeably: sacrifice, victim, offering, satisfaction, priest, ransom, propitiation, payment, lamb. Rather than a developed doctrine, it was more nearly the central proclamation of scriptural truth.

Nevertheless, these elements of Melanchthon's teaching require special mention:

First, this sacrifice was necessary because of God's wrath. Since God had been disobeyed, someone had to suffer the just punishment and curse against sin.

Second, it followed that Christ's sacrifice was to his Father. "This one sacrifice of Christ is a payment, by which Christ offers himself to the eternal Father, and merits reconciliation for us by his obedience." [283] Christ has taken upon himself God's condemnation of sin, and this was the burden he bore upon the cross. The torment came not so much from bodily pain as from the great burden of God's wrath against the sins of humanity, a wrath which Christ knew had been poured out against him, as if he himself had been defiled by all these monstrous crimes.[284]

The first paragraphs of Romans 5 contains many of Melanchthon's favorite verses: "Through him we have obtained access to this grace . . ." (v. 2), ". . . we were reconciled to God by the death of his Son . . ." (v. 10). Throughout his writings he mentioned repeatedly how Christ's sacrifice "placated," "propitiated," or "reconciled" the Father to us. In Christ's offering to his Father he was both priest and sacrifice. Furthermore, as mediator he continues to be our priest and intercessor before God.[285]

Thirdly, Melanchthon believed, this did not mean that Christ acted "independently" of the Father, or that the Father changed his mind from anger to love through Christ's sacrifice. The supposedly inconsistent outlook of the first *Loci* is made clear in Melanchthon's later works. The paradox is that God is a God both of anger and love. Melanchthon prayed thus: "And thou showest thine anger against sin and yet at the same time thy wondrous mercy toward the race of men. . . ." [286] In other words, God does not "change his mind" toward men. The sacrifice is to God, yet God is the one sacrificing his own Son. The cross is a sign both of God's wrath and of his mercy. Only by seeing both sides of God can we come to know him as he truly is, and this is possible only through his Son.

Melanchthon's teaching of the crucifixion has often been compared to that of Anselm of Canterbury,[287] who formulated his theory of the atonement on the basis of God's "honor," which was violated through sin. Punishment for this was taken on by Christ. The similarity between Anselm and Melanchthon derived from two factors. First, they both spoke of Christ's taking, on our behalf, the penalty for sin. Of course Melanchthon didn't need Anselm for this, since it is well founded in the New Testament.

Secondly, both Anselm and Melanchthon tried to summarize Christ's sacrifice logically rather than descriptively, so it is not surprising that Melanchthon's argument runs parallel to that of the great Scholastic teacher.

But there is a profound difference. Anselm's doctrine began from the ontological concept of God's "honor." Melanchthon started from the biblical view of God's wrath. Anselm's line of thought satisfied God's honor with no particular stress on God's love. Melanchthon's entire theology of salvation was founded on the love and mercy of God. Anselm's thought ended with a legalistic, courtroom-like relationship between God and man; Melanchthon ended with a child's faith and trust in a father. Christ's work might have been portrayed similarly, but the view of God was totally different.

The sacrifice of Christ also has another side to it—the motif of victory. Not only had he satisfied the Father, but he had conquered the powers of evil and death.

> The titles of Mediator, King and Savior refer not just to the nature which suffers and dies, but to the victorious person. . . . This person tramples the serpent not only by his merit in the passion but particularly because he conquered death in his body and ours, and restored eternal life and righteousness.[288]

This note from the early Matthew lectures, the so-called "classic" view of the atonement, remained a part of Melanchthon's thought, although subordinate to the sacrificial point of view.

Christ in us

As God's Word, Christ is, of course, still present and working in us. Since the "works of the Trinity outside themselves are indivisible," all three persons are involved in the work, for example, of regeneration. Strictly speaking, Melanchthon maintained, the three persons of the Trinity work in a distinct order, such as "the Father sending the Son, the Son proclaiming consolation, and the Spirit kindling the new actions." [289]

But Melanchthon's faith did not keep to the strict bounds of Trinitarian formulas, so that he spoke almost interchangeably of God, Christ, and the Spirit. One certainly cannot make a distinction between redemption as Christ's work and

sanctification as the Holy Spirit's, since Melanchthon por-
trayed Christ's presence in us as strongly as that of the
Spirit. Indeed, one of his favorite expressions included both:
"Christ renews, sanctifies, and governs *by his Spirit....*" [290]

Christ's presence today has two dimensions, Melanchthon said: his presence in the corporate church and in individual believers. His presence in the church is bound up
with his being God's Word. It began with the first promise
to Adam and Eve, since this Word of promise marks the
beginning of the people of God awaiting his promises.[291] In
the incarnation he came to the church personally: "On this
account, therefore, the Son assumes human nature, because
he was sent to the church directly." [292] Because God called
the church by his Word, we often find in Melanchthon's
works the phrase "the Son gathering the church."

In the *Apology* Melanchthon spoke of the church as the
"kingdom *(regnum)* of Christ," [293] although in other works he
speaks of Christ's kingdom as a spiritual reign not identical
with an institutional church.[294] But everywhere Melanchthon
wrote of Christ as "the head and guardian of the church,
who is forever present with it, keeping and nourishing it." [295]
He described Christ's relationship with his church in profuse
variety: Christ gathers, protects, guards, keeps, restores,
makes alive, sustains, governs, and so on.

Melanchthon laid special emphasis on Christ's concern for
the *ministerium* of the church. This term refers to the *means*
by which he comes to the church, namely the Word and the
Sacraments, but also to the *office* of the ministry, through
which the means of grace are administered. Often Melanchthon will call it the *ministerium* of the Gospel: Christ "him-

self keeps the *ministerium* of the Gospel and is himself working within it." [296] In a sense, he is preserving in the church the *ministerium* of proclamation, presence, and service which he himself carried out on earth.

Concerning Christ's activity in the lives of individual believers, Melanchthon's feelings are best seen, not in his theological writings, but in his letters. He constantly reminded his friends that "Christ takes care of us" [297] or that "Christ keeps us." [298]

> He sits at the right hand of God, that is, he rules with
> the Father, he bears our cares, listens to us, defends us,
> and helps us in all dangers. [299]

One of the dangers of the Swiss rejection of Christ's bodily presence in the Sacrament, according to Melanchthon in the *Apology,* was that to deny full presence was to undermine the whole belief in Christ's presence within us. [300] He had already expressed that concern to Oecolampadius, writing in 1529 that the ancient writings surely intended to include Christ's body in speaking of his presence. [301]

There are, however, some elements about Christ's activity in us which should be clarified. First, the viewpoint of Melanchthon's 1523 *Annotations to John* faded into the background. Christ's *mortificatio* was pictured there as a pattern for the *mortificatio* and humiliation of our lives. The statement which Melanchthon used then—"It is necessary that we conform to his image"—does not appear in his later works. *Mortificatio* becomes a part of *poenitentia,* the sorrow and contrition which come from hearing the Law. [302]

In his later works it has really nothing to do with Christ's own *mortificatio,* humiliation, or suffering.

The concept of Christ as our "example" was also not prominent in Melanchthon's mature years. Christ does not dwell within us for the specific purpose of making us "little Christs," imitators of him. Melanchthon's ethic was not based upon an *imitatio Christi* ("imitation of Christ"). Of course, many of his virtues are those to which Christians aspire, and which he works in us, but Melanchthon never outlined an explicit *imitatio* pattern of life. This was different from Luther, whose writings reflect a strong emphasis on Christ as our example, although, one should add, this emphasis was much stronger in his earlier years than later. Another difference is the way in which the two men described Christ's presence. For Melanchthon, Christ's presence is "working" or "effective" in us; Luther wrote about his simply being within us, a kind of union or intimate fellowship with our person.

It would be tempting, though incorrect, to say that Melanchthon taught *Christus pro nobis* ("Christ for us"), whereas Luther proclaimed *Christus in nobis* ("Christ in us"). It is tempting, for example, to do so on the basis of the letter to Brenz mentioned in the previous chapter, where Melanchthon's focus upon *Christus pro nobis* was in contrast to Luther's strong statement concerning the union of the believer with Christ. And it is true that the two phases did represent differing points of emphases between the two men. Yet the two views are obviously not contradictory, and in fact each man embraced both.

It was this difference, incidentally, which lay at the base

of the distinct manner in which each man presented the doctrine of justification. Our justification, for Luther, was precisely the fact of Christ's uniting himself with us; what he was and did becomes ours when we accept him in faith.[303] His redemptive acts apply to us because we receive him. Melanchthon concentrated more heavily on the benefits of Christ and how they are accounted ours through faith. Here too, these were not two different doctrines of justification, but an example how two men who agreed on a doctrine could add their own insights to it. Melanchthon's Christology pointed toward this doctrine of justification and we also turn to it now.

Justification

One of the conclusions of the first chapter is that Melanchthon had to work out a clear, simple doctrine of justification. His early writings left many questions unanswered and many issues unresolved. In the *Loci* he affirmed the evangelical truth that "Christ is our righteousness" through faith alone, without explaining it further. On the other hand, he wrote that "justification has only begun," leaving us to wonder what justification really is.

In the decade of the 1520's, he sifted his thoughts toward a more thorough explanation. As in other matters, it was the Congress at Augsburg in 1530 which caused him to sum it up. Article 4 of the *Augsburg Confession* is not only the first confessional statement of justification but Melanchthon's own, as well. In his *Apology* exposition he amplified the doctrine.

The brief but concise article on justification in the *Confession* can be divided into three parts:

(a) Our churches also teach that *men cannot be justified before God by their own strength, merits or works*

(b) but are *freely justified for Christ's sake through faith* when they believe that they are received into grace and that their sins are forgiven on account of Christ, who by his death made *satisfaction* for our sins.

(c) *This faith God imputes for righteousness* in his sight (Romans 3, 4).[304]

The first part affirms how we are not justified, guarding the doctrine from misunderstanding. The second part, the heart of the article, binds our salvation to Christ's work. The key words are *gratis . . . propter Christum per fidem* ("freely . . . for Christ's sake through faith"). What is justification? The Latin version of the *Confession* points to two elements: "They are received into grace," and "their sins are forgiven." The German version adds, "become righteous before God by grace" and then summarizes with, "our sin is forgiven, and righteousness and eternal life are given to us."

It is the third part which strikes our eye. The word "impute" was never one of Luther's favorite expressions, and Melanchthon used it sparingly up to 1530.[305] But now it becomes part of the "official" evangelical doctrine. From now on it assumes an increasingly important role in Melanchthon's own thought and ultimately becomes orthodox Lutheran teaching. During the next few years, in the *Apology* and the *Romans Commentary* of 1532, Melanchthon explains its meaning more carefully.

Without doubt, Melanchthon considered justification the critical center of evangelical faith. More than one-fourth of his *Apology* to the *Confession* dealt with the fourth article. He began by calling this matter the "chief doctrine of Christianity," and pinpointed the two great issues at stake:

> . . . when it is properly understood, it illumines and magnifies the *honor of Christ* and brings to pious consciences the *abundant consolation* that they need.[306]

Melanchthon unleashed a broadside against any thought of merit on our part which would contribute to our justification. He reminded his opponents that the Law condemns, and that all their complicated philosophical discussions of man's capacities miss the point: One who seeks salvation on his own merits not only does not seek full refuge in Christ but must be plagued by an uneasy conscience which informs him that his works do not measure up.

Since Roman Catholics opposed the "faith alone" formula of the evangelicals and defined faith in relation to works, Melanchthon spent most of his efforts in an exhausting review of various aspects of faith. He cleared up what he thought were certain misconceptions:

First, faith is "no mere historical knowledge, but the firm acceptance of God's offer promising forgiveness of sins and justification." [307] Of course, faith does include the knowledge of what God and Christ have done, but it embraces more. In the *Confession*, Article 20, Melanchthon had already

written that faith "believes not only the history but also the
effect of the history, namely . . . the forgiveness of sins.
. . ." [308]

About a year after writing the *Apology*, Melanchthon
sharpened his concept of justification even further in his
Romans Commentary of 1532, the work which contains the
most thorough exposition of justification found in his later
works. Here he echoed his first *Loci* and focused on faith
above all as trust *(fiducia)*.[309] *Fiducia* includes knowledge,
but sets the tone where it belongs, on man's new relationship
with God, not on his own works. Melanchthon continued to
use this term throughout all his later works.[310]

Second, Melanchthon clarified one of the problems of the
first *Loci* by asserting that one cannot speak of faith as "the
start of justification or a preparation for justification." [311]
Our justification is not initiated by faith and then perfected
or finished by works. Rather, "by faith itself we are truly
accounted righteous or acceptable before God." [312]

Third, Melanchthon was fond of describing grace, mercy,
and faith as "exclusive" or "exclusive particles." We are
saved by grace *alone,* mercy *alone,* faith *alone.* All other
compromising possibilities are "excluded." The *Formula of
Concord* (Sol. Decl., III, 7, 36) and theologians such as
Martin Chemnitz and Johannes Quenstedt also take up these
two terms, making them a part of standard Lutheran
theology.

Fourth, any kind of a *fides formata charitate* ("faith
formed by love") is out of the question. Faith is a trust and
acceptance of Christ. It is not something which takes shape
by doing works, but which expresses itself in works. Further-

more, Melanchthon cautioned that we are justified *propter Christum* ("on account of Christ, for Christ's sake") not *propter fidem* ("on account of faith . . ."). The proper understanding is *per fidem* ("through faith"), since it is *through faith* or trust that we receive Christ. In the 1535 *Loci,* Melanchthon wrote: "Faith is the means by which the promised mercy for Christ's sake is apprehended." [313]

Still, all these statements are correct: "Faith justifies," "God's mercy justifies," "The promise of God's mercy justifies," etc. In the *Apology* Melanchthon took a step toward explaining this by saying that Paul "correlates and connects promise and faith." [314] In the *Romans Commentary* of 1532 he elaborated this idea.

> Now faith assents to the promises of God and is trust in God's promised mercy. Thus the promised mercy and faith relate to each other as *correlatives.* Therefore, when one says, "Man is justified by faith," your mind should always look for the correlative statement and realize that we are pronounced righteous freely through mercy.[315]

We English-speaking people should note well Melanchthon's precaution here, because our phrase "justified *by* faith" tends to suggest that it is faith which justifies. We are indeed justified "by faith," but this is *correlated* with the fact that it is God's mercy in Christ, received through faith, which justifies. Having once got this straight, however, Melanchthon himself used the various prepositions almost interchangeably—justified *by* faith, *through* faith, *by means of* faith, *by* mercy, *through* mercy, *by means of* mercy, *on account of* mercy, etc.

Imputed and Pronounced

What then *is* justification? In his early works Melanchthon never really explicitly defined it. In the heat of controversy he became more precise. The *Confession* sketched a few elements, as we have seen:

(a) We are received into grace;

(b) Our sins are forgiven;

(c) We become righteous before God by grace;

(d) Righteousness and eternal life are given to us.

In the context of the discussion it is no surprise that the forgiveness of sins became the dominant note in justification. With theology set in the context of Law and Gospel, and man's sin plus God's wrath being the great obstacle to salvation, attention naturally focused upon forgiveness. On occasion Melanchthon narrowed the definition to this: "Justification is the forgiveness of sins. . . . Here we see clearly what justification is. . . ." [316] This emphasis became even more pronounced in the last few years of Melanchthon's life, when he had to defend himself against Andreas Osiander, who held that justification did not include the forgiveness of sins. His defense was carried on by the *Formula of Concord* and later Lutheran theologians, for whom justification was, above all, forgiveness.

But on the whole, Melanchthon never narrowed the definition exclusively to forgiveness. Justification included far more than just that. Another prominent element was reconciliation. He even wrote, "Justification is reconciliation for Christ's sake." [317] But Melanchthon saw forgiveness and reconciliation as practically synonymous and often used them together: ". . . by faith alone we receive the forgiveness of sins and reconciliation for Christ's sake, and reconciliation or justification is something promised because of Christ." [318]

A third term which Melanchthon interchanged with forgiveness and reconciliation to define justification was *acceptatio Dei*, God's acceptance of us. This phrase is found everywhere in the *Romans Commentary:* "Therefore we are righteous . . . by divine acceptance, by which God forgives us our sins." [319]

Actually Melanchthon's concept of justification included all these, and they were most frequently mentioned with each other, in no particular order or sequence. Statements where all these ideas are poured together abound in Melanchthon's writings. For example:

> Justification is the forgiveness of sins, the non-imputation of sin, reconciliation or acceptance, whereby we are accepted by God as righteous through mercy, not on account of our virtues.[320]

If justification and righteousness are synonymous with forgiveness, reconciliation, and acceptance, the next step in Melanchthon's thought had to be an explanation of how these become ours. Here the *Apology* and the *Romans Commentary* represent tremendously significant developments, both for his own teaching and for Lutheran theology.

In the first *Loci* of 1521 Melanchthon had used the word *reputare:* We are "reputed righteous," that is, God reckons or accounts us righteous. This is simply the literal translation of *logizein* in Romans 4:5 (. . . his faith is *reckoned* as righteousness"). This word "repute" is found with monotonous regularity all through Article 4 of the *Apology*, and throughout all the later writings as well.

But followed through logically, "to repute" calls for an object: *What is it* which is reputed as righteousness? Developing this line of thought, Melanchthon began using the word "impute." Whereas "repute" connotes a subjective attitude or mental resolution—God reputes us righteous—"impute" denotes an object: God imputes *something* to us as righteousness. What is this object?

In Article 4 of the *Confession* it was faith which was imputed for righteousness. Also, in the *Apology* Melanchthon used "impute" in his translation of Romans 4:5: "This faith is imputed for righteousness before God." [321] Yet he was too conscious of the tendency to make faith a good work, itself the basis of justification rather than God's mercy and Christ's benefits.

This was why he made such a point of the "correlative" relationship between faith and mercy, to establish God as the one who justifies through faith. To make this point doubly clear, Melanchthon now writes that the imputation of faith is nothing other than the imputation of Christ's righteousness: "Because the righteousness of Christ is given to us through faith, therefore faith is righteousness in us by imputation." [322]

But in the *Apology* he also gave us a glimpse of future trends when he abandoned the imputation of faith for the clear-cut imputation of Christ's righteousness, which happens through faith. We are justified ". . . on account of someone else's righteousness *(propter alienam iustitiam)*, namely Christ's, which is communicated to us through faith." [323]

In the *Romans Commentary* the concept of a *iustitia aliena* —someone else's righteousness imputed to us—was a fixed part of Melanchthon's thought.[324] The term *imputatio iustitiae* ("imputation of [Christ's] righteousness") occurs everywhere. The idea of faith being imputed, as in Article 4 of the *Confession,* is expressed less often, and then as a "correlative" to the *imputatio iustitiae.*

In the years following the *Romans Commentary,* the *imputatio iustitiae* took its place beside the other concepts included in justification. For Melanchthon it was synonymous with forgiveness, reconciliation, and acceptance.[325] All of these concepts describe God's grace to us:

> Now "grace" in Hebrew usage means pardon, mercy, or favor, to be pleasing to, or—as I would say—a gratuitous acceptance. . . . So grace includes these two things: forgiveness of sins and the imputation of righteousness.[326]

These last two received special emphasis in Melanchthon's later years because Andreas Osiander denied them both. It is no wonder, then, that the *Formula of Concord* laid stress on these two elements:

> Our righteousness before God consists in this, that God *forgives* us our sins . . . and *imputes* to us the righteousness of Christ's obedience.[327]

From then on it was only natural that the following generation of Lutheran theologians would concentrate the doctrine of justification particularly on these two beliefs. To be absolutely sure that justification was understood as an act of God toward us, Melanchthon introduced two other terms into his teaching: "pronounce" and "forensic."

> "To be justified" here does not mean that a wicked man is made righteous, but that he is pronounced righteous in a forensic way. . . .[328]

In the *Apology* the word "forensic" was used only these two times, but in later works it appears more frequently; the term *pronuntiare* can be found everywhere, especially in the *Romans Commentary*. Melanchthon illustrated this concept of being pronounced righteous, and innocent by recalling how the Roman people declared Scipio free.[329]

Actually the use of the word "pronounce" did not signify any new shift in Melanchthon's thought. Just as with "forgiveness," "reconciliation," "acceptance," and "imputation," it focused upon justification as God's act, God's decision.[330] The concept reflected the biblical overtone of God's spoken Word as the fiat of his action, beginning with creation. The whole trend of Melanchthon's thought was to make clear that we are justified totally by God, with no contribution whatsoever on our part. What he did was to develop this central doctrine to its logical end, safeguarding it from all directions as well as he could. And in doing so he determined the course of the doctrine among succeeding Lutheran theologians.

Nevertheless, these developments of Melanchthon's thoughts gave his doctrine a distinctive flavor compared with Luther. By basing justification on a pronouncement from God about something outside of us, imputed to us, the whole process acquired a somewhat abstract coloring. In removing justification from any quality or work in us, it tended to become something apart from us altogether. This was certainly not the case with Luther. Justification, for him, was very concrete, a uniting of ourselves with Christ. Luther, of course, agreed in substance with the *imputatio* of Christ's righteousness, since it was his righteousness which God counted as ours, but he never really used the word much himself.[331] Whereas the two Reformers themselves never disputed each other's outlook, scholars today are aware of this shade of difference, feeling that the church has neglected Luther's particular emphasis.

What ultimately happened was that Melanchthon's teaching of justification was given an even more abstract ring by the Lutheran scholars of the next generations—largely an overreaction to Osiander. In the seventeenth century justification became something almost wholly outside of us and sanctification was what took place within us. The two were strictly separated, sowing the seed of much vigorous discussion today.

Melanchthon assuredly had not wanted it that way. Justification was distinct from our good works, but the two were intimately related. Melanchthon's idea of "regeneration" was an important link which held the two together. To this topic we now turn.

Made Righteous and Regenerated

In Melanchthon's early works justification was regarded as regeneration or vivification. This meant that in justifica-

tion something happens to us; we are made alive. This side
of Melanchthon's thinking is reflected in the two most-
discussed and most debated passages of the *Apology:*

> And "to be justified" means to make unrighteous men
> righteous or to regenerate them as well as to be pro-
> nounced or accounted righteous.
> Therefore we are justified by faith alone, justification
> being understood as making an unrighteous man right-
> eous or effecting his regeneration.[332]

These two paragraphs from the *Apology* have spawned
an awesome amount of literature, with dozens of learned
professors taking sides.[333] The underlying assumption of the
whole discussion has been that these statements represent
two doctrines of justification—one a pronounced and imputed
righteousness, the other a righteousness effected or produced
in the believer himself.[334]

The procedure of this controversy has been to give each
side contrasting labels and set them against each other.
Some of the standard labels have been "pronouncing righteous" (*Gerechtsprechung*) versus "making righteous" (*Gerechtmachung*): "synthetic" versus "analytic," and "forensic"
versus "effective." Of course Melanchthon never thought in
such alternatives, and very probably did not anticipate that
such categories would be superimposed on his thinking. He
was a logical man; had he intended to outline "two doctrines
of justification," he would likely have done so. The truth of
the matter is that, for him, "to be made righteous" was the
same as "to be pronounced righteous." Put another way,

to be pronounced righteous was also to be made righteous in God's sight.

The key to understanding this is Melanchthon's use of the word "regeneration." He thought of regeneration and vivification (*regeneratio, vivificatio*) in terms of their literal meanings in Latin: to be born again, to be made alive again. This is precisely what justification does: trusting in Christ, our sins are forgiven, we are reconciled to and accepted by God, who imputes Christ's righteousness to us and pronounces us righteous. This is our justification *and* our regeneration. Being justified before God, we are made alive again. ". . . we are justified, reconciled, and regenerated by faith." [335] It is not something altogether apart from us, for it has a profound, transforming effect within us. In this context Melanchthon could write, "Justification is regeneration." [336]

This is not to say that justification included the good works which followed. Melanchthon was quite clear on that point. But it was not separated from good works either, because this regenerating and vivifying effect of justification was the source of consequent action. In this sense, Melanchthon wrote that justification was both reconciliation *and* "the beginning of our renewal." [337] For him this regeneration was the rebirth from which good works flowed. In the *Apology* article on "penitence" he wrote that "after penitence, that is, conversion or regeneration, must come good fruits and good works." [338]

Though Melanchthon might have opened the door to a more abstract concept of justification with the terms "pronounce" and "impute," he apparently did not intend to make

it less than something effective within the believer by drawing a curtain between it and the restoration of good
works.[339] This trend was given impetus, however, in the
Formula of Concord. In Article 3 the dynamic sense of "regeneration" is separated from justification.[340] Whereas
Melanchthon had intended the idea of "regeneration" to be
the link which intimately relates the two, this term took on
two meanings. This paved the way for the rigidly enforced
separation of justification and sanctification found in Lutheran doctrine of the succeeding centuries.

The New Life

How did Melanchthon portray the new life of this regenerated, justified believer? This is an important question, considering that the young Melanchthon had reflected such
varying opinions. In the Matthew lectures not only the
Christian life but justification itself was obedience to the
Law; in the *Loci* the new life was the spontaneous following of the Spirit's guidance; in the *Annotations to John* it
was following the pattern of Christ's life, with no reference
to the Law.

There are two topics which must be examined here: First,
how does God work this new life in the believer; secondly,
in what way can we speak about this new obedience as
righteousness.

God Working in Us

In the writings which followed the *Apology* the reader
may notice that Melanchthon did not use the term *regener-*

atio as frequently as he did in the *Apology*. Instead, the key word was *simul* ("simultaneously"): "When God forgives sins, *at the same time (simul)* he sends the Holy Spirit, who works in believers new virtues." [341] This emphasis on the *simul*—that all this happens at once—was particularly strong when Melanchthon was accused of separating good works from salvation, or minimizing God's work within us, as was the case in the controversy with Osiander. Justification means simultaneously a new life, all an act of God toward us.

These two dimensions of God's work describe Christian freedom. We are free from sin, first through forgiveness and imputation of righteousness *propter Christum*.[342] "The next step [of Christian freedom] is a gift of the Holy Spirit, through whom believers are made alive, ruled and protected from the fury of the devil." [343]

Both of these embrace the "many-sided variety of Christ's benefits." [344] We have already seen how Melanchthon did not really separate the work of Christ from that of the Holy Spirit. Justification, he said, was a benefit of Christ, but so also in the new life, because "Christ through his Spirit," "the Spirit of Christ," or simply "Christ" continued his strong presence in us.

We have already discussed how Christ works both within the individual believer and within the church as a whole. To make a distinction between Christ who justifies and the Holy Spirit who sanctifies would be a misreading of Melanchthon, since Christ vivifies and frees both in a pronounced, imputed righteousness and in his presence with us.

All this comes into focus in the Lord's Supper. We have seen how Melanchthon was never caught up in the technical debates about the mode of Christ's presence as was Luther. But he never wavered concerning the fact of his presence. We have also seen how a key word in Melanchthon's Christology was *communicatio*—Christ's communicating or sharing of his benefits with us.

Melanchthon's great concern remained the *purpose* and *use* of the Sacrament—its integral part in the believer's new life: "Christ testifies that his *benefit* comes to us, for he gives us his body and binds us to him as his members." [345] In the incarnation the divinity shares *(communicare)* with the humanity in the person of Christ. Now the parallel *communicatio* is the sharing of himself and his benefits with believers.

Melanchthon quoted 1 Corinthians 10:16 literally hundreds of times, in order to direct primary attention to the purpose of the Sacrament:

> The cup of blessing which we bless, is it not a participation in the blood of Christ? The bread which we break, is it not a participation in the body of Christ?

This *communicatio* in the Lord's Supper is the concrete assurance and climax of Christ's working presence in us.

Man's Good Works

During these years the question of the Law lay at the base of much discussion. Because Roman Catholics argued for man's ability to obey the Law and accumulate merit, Melanchthon came to define sin in large part in terms of man's inability to obey the Law. His view of Christ's work

stressed Christ as a sacrifice suffering the penalty of disobedience. The whole issue of righteousness and imputation
led to the problem of man's own subsequent fulfillment of
the Law. The antinomians—those who wished to throw out
the Law altogether—also forced Melanchthon to deal with
the Law.

All these factors made it inevitable that Melanchthon
would also speak about the Christian life in terms of the
Law. We have seen how he gradually abandoned an ethic
oriented around an *imitatio Christi*. But if Christ's life is not
the pattern for Christian living, what is? The answer is good
works, or more specifically, works according to the Law.

Article 6 of the *Confession* outlined Melanchthon's
thought: (a) faith inevitably produces good works; (b)
good works are necessary because of God's command and
will, and (c) yet they do not justify us.[346]

In the *Apology* Melanchthon explained this "new obedience" in greater detail, especially in the section on "Love
and the Keeping of the Law." [347] In answer to the Catholics,
who had charged that "justification through faith" resulted
in promiscuous license, he replies that "the keeping of the
Law should begin in us and increase more and more." [348]

This led Melanchthon to the term "the third use of the
Law" as a guide for Christian life.[349] Luther himself never
used the term, although anyone who reads his Catechism
exposition of the Commandments can see that he agreed in
substance with Melanchthon. The phrase "third use of the
Law" was later endorsed in the *Formula of Concord,* when
it became a standard Lutheran concept. The term has stirred
up much discussion today as the result of current Luther

research. But Melanchthon, too, was aware of some of the dangers of an overemphasis on Law in the Christian life.

Melanchthon conceded that good works and obedience to the Law please God. But he was quick to add that works in themselves neither pleased nor satisfied God; only because we have first been justified through Christ are they pleasing to him.[350] In his later work he put it this way: "Therefore after *the person* is pleasing [to God through faith] then also are the works pleasing." [351] He would not compromise the fact that we are accepted by God only through Christ.

Yet when a believer obeys the Law, his obedience does constitute "righteousness." This righteousness of works must inevitably follow the imputed righteousness of Christ:

> Although a person receives the forgiveness of sins for Christ's sake through mercy and is righteous, that is, accepted, nevertheless a righteousness of works must surely follow.[352]

Indeed, "good works are necessary and they are a righteousness of law," or as Melanchthon more often wrote, "a righteousness of works." [353] Both Luther and Melanchthon spoke of these "two kinds of righteousness"—of faith and of works.[354]

But it is obvious that Melanchthon was uneasy when he spoke of a "righteousness of works in the same breath as the "righteousness of faith." "I do concede" he admitted, "that two kinds of righteousness are necessary, a righteousness of faith and a righteousness of works." [355] But he never mentioned the second without taking meticulous care to put it in its proper perspective: We can speak of a righteousness of works only because the *believing person* has first been accounted righteous in faith.[356]

Melanchthon constantly repeated that our own works are not worthy of salvation, and that we remain sinners even after justification. He never used Luther's phrase *simul iustus et peccator,* but he repeatedly employed the words "even though," "even if," "although"—"we receive reconciliation . . . *even though* sin still remains in our flesh." [357] Any righteousness in our works is thus never more than "weak and impure." [358] In and by itself it could not stand as truly righteous. "Therefore it does not please God for its own sake, and it is not acceptable for its own sake." [359] Ultimately, all righteousness is a work and gift of God. So the whole topic of the "two kinds of righteousness" can in no way exalt our own goodness but "teaches us our weakness and illuminates the beneficium Christi." [360]

CHAPTER FOUR

Controversialist

Students of church history usually first become acquainted with Melanchthon as a footnote to Luther, and then come to know him only as the author of the *Confession* and the man who got himself into all kinds of arguments after Luther died. This is correct; the 14 years of Melanchthon's life after Luther's death were racked with controversy, most of which shook the whole evangelical church and were settled only after the arduous negotiations leading to the *Formula of Concord.*

But history students seldom learn Melanchthon's own position in these matters. The controversies usually went far beyond the bounds of his actual opinions. They were fought between the "Philippists" or "Melanchthonians," who misrepresented Melanchthon, and the "Genuine-Lutherans," who misrepresented Luther. This chapter, therefore, will attempt to sketch Melanchthon's own teachings in these matters.

The Adiaphoristic Controversy

This battle grew out of the "Leipzig Interim," the settlement imposed upon the Saxon evangelicals following their defeat by the emperor in 1546. Melanchthon was persuaded to go along with concessions in what he termed "indifferent" or "external" things *(adiaphora)* and did not stand in defiance of the changes forced on his church during the interim.

The details of the strife are a matter of church history and cannot be reviewed here.[361] There are, however, two things which should be mentioned.

First, looking back we see that Melanchthon misjudged history. He feared—and being overly apprehensive was one of his life-long characteristics—that without concessions the emperor would cruelly stamp out the evangelical faith in Saxony, similar to what took place in Swabia.

He therefore calculated that they might be able to preserve the chief doctrine of their faith, justification by grace through faith, if they conceded to the emperor these "external things." Under normal circumstances he would not have compromised, but he felt the very existence of the evangelical cause was at stake.

However, the evangelicals regained their sovereignty in the Peace of Augsburg in 1555, and the threat was over. Melanchthon would not have needed to concede anything. Instead of going down in history as a diplomat who preserved the church, he appeared to have been cowardly. Even he realized and admitted afterward that he should not have been so apprehensive and should have handled the whole matter differently.

Secondly, the theological question of *adiaphora* needs continual re-examination. The *Formula of Concord* sternly rapped any changes or concessions whatsoever, even in so-called *adiaphora,* when such are forced under pressure or threat. In that setting it was a sound and wise decision, but the church must continue to ask itself what is essential, what can or should be changed, and under what circumstances change is beneficial. George Calixtus tried in the next century to define the "essential" and "nonessential," but was not widely accepted by the Lutheran Church. Now in our "ecumenical age," when we are drawing nearer to other churches, the question of "indifferent" and "external" things and nonessentials reappears in an entirely new light.

In reviewing this controversy we would do well to see not only the negative prohibition of concession under pressure, but also the positive side:

> We believe, teach, and confess that the community of God in every locality and every age has authority to change such ceremonies according to circumstances, as it may be most profitable and edifying to the community of God.[362]

The tone of this article is not one of obstructionism against all change, but of fidelity to the Gospel. *Adiaphora* are precisely those "ceremonies or church usages which are neither commanded nor forbidden in the Word of God." [363] While we cannot be forced to change these external things, neither can we allow them to stand in the way of fellowship. The important issue lies not with these externals, but with the Gospel.

The controversy itself belongs to history, but the decision of the *Formula of Concord* provides ecumenical insight for our day. The great issue is faith in the Gospel and use of the sacraments.[364] Let us concentrate our efforts here, and when accord is reached, the *adiaphora* must not stand in the way.

The Majoristic Controversy

Here is a classic example of how two parties who intensely dislike each other almost deliberately misunderstand the other and inflate a question into an excessively distorted battle. George Major, a friend and former student of Melanchthon, wanted to emphasize the fact that faith must inevitably produce good works, and he stated, "Good works are necessary for salvation." [365] If one understands the statement correctly, it is not un-evangelical, but it is unwise to defend a thesis so open to misunderstanding. Melanchthon advised his friend to drop it, but Major persisted.

Nicholas von Amsdorf, Lutheran bishop of Magdeburg who had mistrusted Melanchthon for years, rose up in angry disagreement. Instead of illuminating the discussion with balanced insight, Amsdorf flung himself to the even more foolish opposite extreme and affirmed that "good works are detrimental and injurious to salvation." As with Major's thesis, its intention was correct—reliance and trust on good works are detrimental to salvation—but it almost begged misinterpretation.

Though Major was a "Philippist," Melanchthon himself was not involved in the debate, and its conclusion did not reflect upon his own theology. The *Formula of Concord,*

Article 4 ("Good Works"), wisely rejected both statements and set the whole discussion right again.

The Synergistic Controversy

The question of natural man's capacity—the capacity of his will, reason, etc.—has always been a touchy issue for Protestants. Both Catholics and Humanists thought of man as capable of certain religious attainments. We have seen how Melanchthon shared with Luther the strong rejection of man's ability to know, believe, or obey God in any way, and yet was Humanist enough to fear any traces of determinism which diminished a sense of man's responsibility. This controversy hinged on the question of the ability of man's will to "cooperate" with God. The name comes from 2 Corinthians 6:1: "Working together (*synergos*) with him. . . ."

The debate was launched with Melanchthon's mention of "three causes—the Word, the Holy Spirit, and man's will, which is not idle but assenting." In the 1535 *Loci* he spoke of the doubts which often assail a striken conscience, advising the believer to hold fast to the promises of God. "In this case," he continued, "we see three causes joined together—the Word, the Holy Spirit, and the will, surely not idle, but fighting against its infirmity." [366]

In the last *Loci* edition of his lifetime, written in 1559, Melanchthon set this concept in the context of good actions: "When we begin from the Word, three causes of good actions come together—the Word of God, the Holy Spirit, and the human will, which does not oppose but assents to the Word of God." [367]

Looking carefully at these passages, it is apparent that we

are not dealing with the first moment of conversion, but with aspects of the ongoing Christian life. No one disputed that man's will is active in the Christian, preceded and guided by the first two "causes," nor did Luther voice disagreement with Melanchthon's statement.

It was the passage from the *Examen Ordinandorum* of 1554 which drew the heavy fire, since it speaks specifically about conversion:

> Therefore in conversion three causes join together—the Word of God, the Holy Spirit, whom the Father and the Son send that our hearts might be kindled, and our assenting will, which does not reject the Word of God.[368]

This caused many lifted eyebrows, because any thought of man's being able to contribute to his own conversion was anathema to the evangelicals. But to understand the paragraph as Melanchthon meant it, his opponents should have read farther to the section "Concerning Repentance" (De Poenitentia). There he defines repentance as "conversion to God, which contains sorrow and consolation, or mortification and vivification. . . ."[369] Repentance or conversion includes "contrition . . . to accept by faith in Christ the forgiveness of sins, reconciliation, justification, and vivification, and to begin new obedience."[370]

In other words, Melanchthon's idea of conversion was the life-long process of continually repenting, turning to God, being justified, and obeying. It was not limited—as it was in later usage—to the first moment of "conversion," when faith in the believer is first worked by God. It would, of course,

be quite "un-Lutheran" to say that the human will contrib-
utes to or is a cause of the first moment of conversion, but
Melanchthon neither said nor intended to say that. In his
writings he was unbendingly explicit in denying man any
ability to believe in God on his own. But after God has
"converted" him, then the believer's will must be actively
guided by the Spirit.

In February 1557 Melanchthon wrote a letter to Duke
John Albert of Magdeburg, replying to these attacks.[371] First
he flatly rejected all "stoic" and determinist trends. Then he
wrote:

> . . . As far as spiritual actions are concerned—true
> knowledge of God, faith, prayer, patience, perseverance
> —it is certain that the human will *cannot will* or *accom-*
> *plish anything by its own powers, unless God himself*
> *first comes to it through Word,* effecting divine inspira-
> tion and inciting the will to assent and obey.
>
> *After* this motion and impulse is accomplished *by the*
> *divine will,* then the human will is not simply passive.
> Moved and supported by the Holy Spirit, the will does
> not refuse, but assents and obeys God. It cooperates,
> *sunergos esti,* as Paul says. . . .

One can fault Melanchthon, however, for not anticipating
how easily his "conversion" passage would be misunderstood.
In none of those "three causes" paragraphs did he really
pause to explain precisely what he meant. It is no wonder
that many of his more "liberal" friends used such passages
to support their "un-Lutheran" views of the will's ability,
even in the initial conversion. The "Genuine-Lutheran"

opponents of these "Philippists" then automatically included Melanchthon with the others.

The *Formula of Concord* soundly rejected all synergistic tendencies. Since it understood "conversion" as the beginning of faith, it also implied a rejection of Melanchthon. Actually, it did not repudiate Melanchthon's views, but the caricatures which had been made of them both by Melanchthon's friends and his enemies.[372]

The Crypto-Calvinist Controversy

This issue concerned the Lord's Supper. It was so named because the "Genuine-Lutherans" feared that some Lutherans were, under the surface, "secretly" *(crypto)* more Calvinist than Lutheran. They were correct; some of Melanchthon's students drifted into a Calvinist conception of the Lord's Supper. They were also correct in charging that Melanchthon himself had displayed distinctive ideas about the Supper. Lumping him with the crypto-Calvinists, they accused him too of being "un-Lutheran," of betraying Luther's convictions.

There were both theological and practical sides to Melanchthon's position. Let us outline each.

The theological question revolved around his concept of the *communicatio idiomatum.* In the previous chapter we demonstrated how he saw the two natures of Christ united in the person of Christ. From the beginning of the incarnation into eternity the attributes of each nature are joined to the *concrete person* of Christ. Whatever he does for and with us, he does as this incarnated, God-man person. When we speak of him, therefore, we speak of the person. One can, of course, speak about each nature *abstractly*, but that has little purpose, since the nature does not exist abstractly but as a part of the concrete person. Not only that, it invites all sorts of pointless speculating.

In technical language, this means that Melanchthon never spoke in terms of the *genus majestaticum*, where the attributes specifically of the divine nature are communicated to the human nature. We can only conjecture what Melanchthon might have said about this third *genus* as outlined in the *Formula*. But he might have said that such discourse clouds the vital distinction between the natures, puts the discussion into scripturally unwarranted categories, is too abstract, and unnecessarily bypasses the united, concrete person of Christ. He also disliked the term "physical ubiquity" of Christ, since this, again, called attention to one particular nature, apart from the whole person.[373] Luther, on the other hand, spoke very much in this vein, largely to emphasize once and for all the presence of the human nature in the Lord's Supper. This meant that Melanchthon felt it was sufficient to affirm that the whole *person* of Christ is present, which, of course, includes both natures. In the same letter to Duke John Albert cited in the previous section he wrote:

> About the Lord's Supper we believe and confess that when it is administered as Christ instituted it, Christ— God and man—is truly present. . . . The body and blood of our Lord Jesus Christ are truly and substantially received.[374]

He wrote to the city of Wesel in 1556 that the essential belief in the Supper is that "Christ is present substantially and effectively." [375] He constantly affirmed the presence of Christ and of his body and blood—truly, substantially, effectively, really—but he drew the line at isolating one nature from the other and speaking about "the presence of the human nature" by itself. Having accepted the union of the two natures in the incarnation, any further talk of just one nature in Christ's acts was for him redundant.

Melanchthon's practical concerns also colored his doctrine. In almost every instance where he discussed the Lord's Supper he moved from the affirmation of Christ's presence to his primary interest, the *purpose* of the Sacrament. [376] In about 1551 he wrote a "Summary" of his convictions, insisting that two things must be held fast. The first was the presence: "(1) That in the giving of the bread and wine the body and blood of Christ are given to those partaking." [377] From that brief statement he went into the purpose: "(2) That this partaking has been instituted primarily to confirm faith, because it is a testimony that Christ has joined us to himself as members." [378]

Melanchthon felt that the endless discussion about the mode of Christ's presence had obscured the real issue: the purpose of the Supper. He hoped that by stating the truth of the real and substantial presence of Christ's whole person one might leave it at that and go on to the important thing.

We have already seen how he constantly tried to focus attention on 1 Corinthians 10:16, where the Supper is a sharing *(koinonia-communicatio)* of Christ's body and blood. This "sharing-participation-fellowship" concept was for him the great truth of the Sacrament: ". . . in this Sacrament Christ imparts (*communicat*) his body to us, and testifies that we are members of his body, in which he is effectively working." [379]

He insisted that all reference to Christ's presence be centered in the celebration of the Sacrament, and that all speculation about the continuing presence of Christ in the bread and wine after the Eucharist was irreverent. Christ is present in *usu sacramenti*, "in the practice or celebration of the Sacrament," not *extra usum*, "apart from the celebration." [380] He pointed to the words of institution, which referred to the action of the Sacrament: "*Take, eat*, this is my body." [381] He intensely abhorred the *Corpus Christi* procession, where the bread was paraded around, supposedly still as Christ's body, long after the celebration was ended. This was idolatry, he said, because adoration of Christ was replaced by adoration of the bread.[382] Again, he directed attention to the pastoral function of the Sacrament: "Christ is present for the sake of men, not for the sake of bread." [383]

Melanchthon also avoided an *inclusio localis*, the view that Christ's body was limited to and within the bread. First, the Word of God, the Son, cannot be limited to one place. Secondly, and even more important, the term *in pane*, "in the bread," opened the door to such unedifying speculations as whether or not Christ's body is chewed, swallowed, and digested.[384] Again, this sort of thing was irreverent and clouded the true purpose of the Sacrament. Melanchthon felt it was sufficient to declare that in receiving the bread and wine we receive Christ's body and blood. For this reason he preferred the phrase *cum pane*, "with the bread": "This partaking was instituted, in which the Son of God is truly and substantially present *with* the bread and wine." [385] The term "with" eliminated the technicalities but still focused the presence of Christ on the elements of bread and wine. In the version of the *Confession* which he wrote in 1540 *(Variata)* he stated that, ". . . the body and blood of Christ are truly given *with* the bread and wine to those partaking in the Lord's Supper."

Since Luther had used the terms "in and under" in the *Large Catechism* and elsewhere, many thought that the preposition "with" was meant to express Melanchthon's disagreement with Luther. Actually, because both affirmed the true and substantial presence of Christ, it was not a question of disagreement; rather, it reflected the fact that Luther's argument was directed primarily against the Zwinglians, Enthusiasts, and Baptists, whereas Melanchthon directed most of his fire against the Roman Catholic view. The *Formula of Concord* simply combined all three—in, with, and under—a phrase which has been handed down in Catechism classes for more than four centuries.[386]

There was also a shade of difference in Luther's and Melanchthon's concept of the *manducatio impiorum,* "oral reception by the unbeliever." Luther asserted that not only the "unworthy" *(indigni)* receive the body and blood of Christ, but that Christ so binds himself to the elements that even unbelievers *(impii)* receive his body and blood. In his struggle against the left wing of the Reformation, Luther wanted to establish that Christ's presence was not something which our faith produces, but was wholly Christ's act. Melanchthon, on the other hand, directing his arguments more toward the Catholic side, was afraid of an attitude which made the Sacrament appear much like an act of magic totally apart from the believer's faith. Like Luther, Melanchthon strongly endorsed the *manducatio indignorum,* the teaching that an unworthy believer received Christ, according to 1 Corinthians 11:27 f. But since he was preoccupied with the purpose of the Lord's Supper—the effective presence of Christ among believers—he was thinking a priori in the context of faith and had no reason to discourse about the *manducatio impiorum.* Though he did not deny it, neither had he any compulsion to deal with it.

In view of all this, was Melanchthon's mature teaching concerning the Supper "Lutheran"? Or was he really closer to Calvin, or between Calvin and Luther, as his opponents charged? When one realizes that Calvin's leading motif was Christ's *spiritual* presence mediated by the Holy Spirit, Melanchthon was decidedly "Lutheran." There was never a hint of just a "spiritual" presence, and the Holy Spirit was present not only "effectively," that is, working in us, but also "substantially," by his body and blood.

Still, it was inevitable that Melanchthon's views would play a part in this controversy. Fearing as he did the extremes on the "right," such as Roman Catholic transubstantiation, and not, therefore, precisely echoing Luther's strong feeling toward the "physical" presence and the reception of unbelievers, it is no wonder that he was regarded by crypto-Calvinists as a kindred spirit. The crypto-Calvinists on the left and the Genuine-Lutherans on the right both seized upon this difference in outlook between Melanchthon and

Luther, so that Melanchthon's whole position in its proper context was no longer heard.

The *Formula of Concord* carefully and thoroughly affirmed Luther's outspoken stand against the Swiss and the Sacramentarians. This was not surprising since, like Luther, the authors set out explicitly to define the Lutheran position against the left wing and Reformed opinions.[387] Of course they also rejected the Roman Catholic doctrine in passing, [388] but the bulk of their argument was directed against the left.

The Osiandrian Controversy

The controversy with Andreas Osiander deserves special mention because current Luther research has reopened the question once again.[389] It was also a struggle in which, ironically, Melanchthon and the Genuine-Lutherans found themselves on the same side, a coalition which had a decisive effect on Lutheran theology.

Osiander was an early follower of Luther and was convinced that Luther's interpreters, above all Melanchthon, were not reflecting the Reformer's whole faith. In his attempts to fill in what he held essential, he developed peculiar opinions which led to his almost unanimous condemnation from all sides.

There was a mystical side to Osiander which was shared neither by Melanchthon nor the conservative Lutherans. This mysticism colored his teaching, particularly in his doctrine of the "Word of God," his central theme. The proclamation of the Christian message, Osiander said, was in outward words, but within this proclamation was also the "inward

Word," the Word, or Son of God, working through the outward word. To receive the Word of God was to receive
Christ in the heart. Faith was simply this indwelling of
Christ. It followed that where Christ was, there was also
his righteousness. We are therefore justified when through
faith Christ's righteousness dwells within us and is accounted by God as our righteousness.[390]

Thus far Osiander's position sounds not only sensible and
evangelical, but also is similar to Luther's. Indeed, Osiander
correctly argued that his teaching contained insights of
Luther which Melanchthon had not stressed—justification
and the reception of Christ within the believer. It would
have been best for the church if the two men could have
amicably enriched each other's theology, but that didn't
happen. From his Interim-caused exile in Königsberg,
Osiander leveled bitter attacks on Melanchthon. The whole
discussion turned into a confusion of misunderstanding on
both sides.

Osiander drew two further conclusions which were so
soundly rejected that his worthwhile insights were also
washed away. First, he reasoned that if justification were
limited to the indwelling of Christ, then Christ's redemptive
work on earth was little more than a prelude or necessary
prerequisite of justification. He separated "redemption," as
he called Christ's earthly work, from "justification."

That led him to the logical conclusion that *all* men are
redeemed, since Christ died for all, but not all are justified.
Because all are redeemed, all can be justified if they receive
him. We are not justified by what Christ *does*, but by what

he *is;* by receiving his person, we receive his essence, which is righteousness, and we are then justified.

This reflects, of course, the mystic in him, since mystics have little use for the historical dimension of the faith. Just as this affirmation drew fire from Melanchthon and others, so it would surely have been denounced by Luther. The Reformer's idea of justification was the reception of Christ, but it was intimately bound up with Christ's mission and sacrifice on earth. Luther made no distinction between what Christ did and what he was.

Second, Osiander was a fine Old Testament scholar and decided that the doctrine of justification was essentially the same in both Testaments. Believers in those times were justified because God's righteousness dwelt with them. Specifically, this was the righteousness of the Logos, the Word of God, or the second person of the Trinity. If this was true before the incarnation, then it followed that even after the union of the divine and human natures in Christ, it was still the righteousness of the Logos, the divine nature of Christ only, which justified us. Christ's human nature was of course active in redemption, but played no role in justification.

Luther assuredly would not have accepted that, and neither did anybody else except for a few scattered defenders. The *Formula of Concord* (Articles 3 and 8) flatly repudiated both these conclusions of Osiander and took no account of what was worthwhile in his views.

The tragedy of the controversy was that the important issue soon became so distorted with slogans and misunderstandings that the discussion disintegrated into loud but empty volleys. Neither side really understood the other, nor tried very hard to. Osiander accused Melanchthon of teaching only a "Gerechtsprechung" (pronouncing righteous), and Melanchthon caricatured Osiander's ideas as "Gerechtmachung" (making righteous), whereas neither slogan really fit either side. The opposite sides were also labeled as advocating "imputed" or "effective" righteousness, whereas in reality they both included each.

Melanchthon insisted that Osiander was sliding back into Catholicism, which was not so. Osiander charged Melanchthon with leaving Christ out of the Christian life, which was not so. Melanchthon wrote that Osiander taught work righteousness, which was not so. Osiander said that Melanchthon's concept of faith was devoid of content, which was not so. On and on it went.

The controversy had a subtle but profound effect both on Melanchthon and on subsequent Lutheran theology. Melanchthon's great fear concerning Osiander was that the description of justification as Christ's being and working in us could easily be interpreted to include those works which this produces. Therefore he emphasized twice as emphatically the "imputed righteousness" and regarded the indwelling of Christ more and more as a result of this justification. This again tended to make justification abstract, something which takes place apart from and outside of us rather than something God does to us or works within us. This gave impetus to the development in Lutheran theology which separated justification so completely from sanctification that faith was too easily divorced from life. Neither Melanchthon nor the other theologians intended this to be the case, but the polemics, first against the Roman Catholics and then against Osiander, pulled their theology in that direction.

Osiander's position was that justification and sanctification were distinct but not separated: that which justifies us also sanctifies us, namely Christ within us. Justification and new life come from the indwelling of Christ in our hearts. If only Osiander had not been consumed in the polemics which muddled his central message! To be sure, the "winners" of the controversy, Melanchthon and the Genuine-Lutherans, held to Christ's work in both justification and sanctification, but the first was by imputation and the second by indwelling. The force of Luther's and Osiander's integral view was diminished.

Several centuries removed from the bitterness the strife caused, we can look back and give credit to Osiander for his central insight, regretting the fateful course he chose during the battle. Perhaps the controversy can teach us a valuable lesson for our ecumenical age: Polemics of slogans and caricatures cause both sides to lose; even among those who profoundly disagree, dialogue in a brotherly spirit can be mutually enriching.

Abbreviations and Editions Used

CR *Corpus Reformatorum. Philippi Melanthonis Opera,* Halle, 1834-1860.

StA *Studienausgabe—Melanchthons Werke,* ed. by Robert Stupperich. Gütersloh: Gerd Mohn, 1952-.

LW *Luther's Works*—American Edition, ed. by Jaroslav Pelikan and Helmut T. Lehmann. St. Louis: Concordia Publishing House, and Philadelphia: Fortress Press, 1955-.

WA (Weimar Ausgabe) *D. Martin Luthers Werke. Kritische Gesamtausgabe.* Weimar, 1883-.
References are made to the volume (Roman numerals) and the page, plus, in the case of StA and WA, to the line on the page.

References to the Lutheran Confessions are taken from *The Book of Concord,* ed. by Theodore G. Tappert. Philadelphia: Muhlenberg Press, 1959. For easy reference to the original editions or other translations, paragraph numbers are also included with the page.

Selected Writings *Melanchthon—Selected Writings,* ed. by Elmer Flack and Lowell Satre. Minneapolis: Augsburg Publishing House, 1962.

Bacc. Theses *Baccalaureate Theses* of September, 1519, in *Selected Writings,* pp. 17f.

Paul and the Scholastics In *Selected Writings,* pp. 31f.

Matthew *Annotationes in Evangelium Matthaei* of 1519-1520, StA IV, 134f.

Loci *Loci Communes* of 1521, CR XXI, 81f., and StA II, 3f. (Quoted from StA II.)

John *Annotationes in Evangelium Joannis* of 1523, CR XIV, 1047f.

Confession *Augsburg Confession,* quoted from *The Book of Concord,* Tappert ed.

Apology *Apology* of the *Augsburg Confession,* quoted in *The Book of Concord,* Tappert ed.

Romans Com. *Commentarii in Epistolam Pauli ad Romanos* of 1532, StA V, 25f.

1535 Loci *Loci Communes* of 1535, CR XXI, 334f.

Examen *Examen Ordinandorum* of 1554, CR XXIII, 1f.

1555 Loci *Loci Communes* of 1555, translated into English by Clyde Manschreck, *Melanchthon on Christian Doctrine,* New York: Oxford University Press, 1965.

Explicatio *Explicatio Symboli Niceni* of 1557, CR XXIII, 355f.

1559 Loci *Loci Communes* of 1559, CR XXI, 601f., and StA II, 165f. (Quoted from StA II.)

Notes

Chapter I. REFORMER

1. Henry Osborn Taylor writes, for example: "It seems safe to say that no man had done as much to prepare the mind of Europe for religious reformation as Erasmus of Rotterdam." *Erasmus and Luther.* New York: Collier, 1962, p. 59.

2. For an historical account of Melanchthon's position between Erasmus and Luther, cf. Wilhelm Maurer's chapter, "Melanchthons Anteil am Streit zwischen Luther und Erasmus," *Melanchthon-Studien.* Gütersloh: Verlagshaus Gerd Mohn, 1964, pp. 137f.

3. From Melanchthon's lecture on January 25, 1520, entitled *Paul and the Scholastics,* in *Melanchthon: Selected Writings,* translated by Charles Leander Hill, ed. by Elmer E. Flack and Lowell Satre. Minneapolis: Augsburg Publishing House, 1962, p. 42.

4. Melanchthon writes approvingly of the Platonists: "Even the Platonists saw that the minds of men needed a certain internal catharsis, as they called it, that is, a cleansing, without which they denied that solid virtue would be established." *Ibid.,* p. 39.

5. Melanchthon speaks both as a Humanist and Reformer of the "frivolous opinion of those who consign the doctrine of Paul to the limits of one age and who foolishly hold that it was written to Christians who were still unpolished, whereas there is now need of a more sublime theology for those fully developed. For in that age particularly . . . the celestial Spirit, who alone reveals the hidden mysteries of Scripture, was more familiar to their pure minds." *Ibid.,* pp. 42f.

6. Cf. Luther's letters to Spalatin (August 3, 1518) and Johann Lang (September 9, 1518). *WA Briefe,* Vol. I, p. 92.

7. Melanchthon's usual title is even more inclusive: *Praeceptor Germaniae,* "Teacher of Germany," a tribute to his pioneering work in reorganizing the German school system.

    The first *Loci* edition and the two later revised editions are published in the *Corpus Reformatorum* (CR), Vol. 21. The first (1521) and the last (1559) editions have been published in *Melanchthons Werke—Studienausgabe* (StA), edited by Robert Stupperich. Gütersloh: Verlagshaus Gerd Mohn, 1952, Vol. II. The first *Loci* was translated into English by Charles Leander Hill (Boston, 1944). References will be given from StA II, page and line, although Dr. Hill's translation was also occasionally consulted.

    Loci Communes literally means "common, general topics." The best English equivalent would perhaps be "main issues" or "basic issues."

8. StA II., p. 6, line 31.

9. *Ibid.,* p. 7, lines 12-19.

10. In his *Operationes in Psalmos* of 1519-1521 Luther writes, "To know Christ is to know the cross and to understand God through the crucified flesh of Christ." (WA 5, 108, 9f. : *Sed Christum nosse est Crucem nosse est deum sub carne crucifixa intelligere.*) Erich Vogelsang claims

141

that the source of Melanchthon's phrase can be traced as far back as Luther's first lectures on the psalms. *Die Anfänge von Luthers Christologie.* Berlin: W. de Gruyter & Co., 1929, p. 159. Cf. pp. 11 f.

11. Prof. Maurer writes, "When Melanchthon seeks to know Christ only in his *beneficia (Wohltaten)*, he is adopting a principle of Erasmus, who termed it an impiety to inquire into matters 'which one does not need to know for salvation.'" *Melanchthon-Studien, op. cit.,* p. 110.

    Erasmus uses the term *beneficia* as the Latin translation of God's grace, *charis. Paraphrases in Novum Testamentum,* Vol. 3, Berlin, pp. 267, 268, 303. It is also equivalent to God's love, *agape, ibid.,* p. 264. Cf. also *Ratio seu Methodus, in Ausgewählte Werke,* ed. by Hajo Holborn. Munich: C. H. Beck, 1933, pp. 213, 5 f., 11, 13 f., 20 f. A few times the term is used in specific context with Christ's redemptive work: "The benefit of God is thus bestowed, so that the accumulated sin of all people might be abolished by Christ's death." *Paraphrasis* to Romans, *ibid.,* p. 267. Cf. p. 265.

12. In his early writings Melanchthon used the phrase much like Erasmus. His *Theologica Institutio,* very likely written in the summer of 1519, reflects this view. CR 21, 51. Cf. also his lectures on the Gospel of Matthew from the winter of 1519-1520. StA IV, 152, 15 f. On the other hand, in these same Matthew lectures we find the term used in the same sense as in the *Loci,* StA II, 170, 11 f.

13. *Matthew,* StA IV, 148, 20 f.

14. *Paul and the Scholastics,* p. 35.

15. *Ibid.*

16. "For it is not within our power to drive away from their own kingdom the passions of sin which occupy an abode deep within the soul like some impregnable fortress where they exercise their tyranny over all our members. . . . Some of the ancients thought that reason in man functions like a charioteer and called the passions horses. But reason is conquered by passion. Holding the reins in vain, the charioteer is borne on by the horses. Nor does the team heed curb. Rather the passions shake off reason in the same way that the horses of the sun's chariot did Phaeton. This power of sin is conquered by the grace of Christ alone." *Ibid.,* p. 39.

    "A sewer of such a nature is the mind of man, on every side festering with all the most poisonous passions." *Ibid.* "We are so dragged away to vices that by no counsel of our own, by no powers of our own, can we be called back from them. *Ibid.,* p. 35. Not even Luther spoke more strongly than this.

17. *Loci,* StA II, p. 9, lines 5 f.

18. *Ibid.,* p. 9, lines 7 f.

19. *Ibid.,* p. 9, lines 24 f. ". . . and just as the senate in a republic is enslaved to a tyrant, so is man's reason servile to the will." *Ibid.*

20. Nominalism was the school of thought which felt that man's will held sway over his reason. Melanchthon, as Luther, was familiar with the long-standing disputes between the Rationalists and Universalists against the Nominalists, but was not greatly interested in the intricacies

of the discussion. Both men, though surely subconsciously influenced by this side of Nominalism, preferred to base their teaching on scriptural evidence rather than the arguments current among philosophers.

21. *Ibid.*, StA II p. 13, lines 11 f. "Affections," *affectus* means the drives and appetites of man, likes and dislikes, etc.

22. "Furthermore, why not substitute the term 'heart' for the 'will'? For Scripture calls the heart the most powerful part of man, that part in which the affections originate." (*Ibid*, p. 13, lines 20 f.) Cf. p. 15, lines 28 f. Melanchthon's view of the affections is a remarkable foreshadowing of modern psychology's discovery of the subconscious, that man is molded and controlled by something deep within him, more profound than either reason or will—whether it be called the subconscious or the affections!

23. *Ibid.*, p. 18, lines 38 f.

24. *Ibid.*, p. 18, lines 7 f. Cf. p. 38, line 26.

25. "Original sin is an inherent inclination, a certain inborn impulse and drive, by which we are drawn into sin." *Ibid.*, p. 17, lines 32 f.
We find this already in the Matthew lectures: "For we are constantly seized by a congenital disease, contracted from the sin of Adam, which is a certain innate inclination (*propensio*) within our members toward sinning, so that no one can control his affections by his own nature." *Matthew*, p. 135, lines 13 f.

26. *Loci*, p. 21, lines 28 f.

27. At the end of the section Melanchthon lists summary statements, among which are these (*Ibid.*, p. 38, lines 30 f.):
3. Since the Spirit of God is no longer in men, man knows, loves, and strives toward nothing but carnal things.
5. Thus it follows that man through his natural powers can do nothing but sin.
7. Since Scripture testifies that the heart is impure, it follows that all human capacities are impure.
8. For the heart does not signify only the sensual appetite, as some Scholastics have called it, but the seat of all affections—of love, hate, blasphemy, and unbelief.

28. Melanchthon had begun his argument by eliminating the whole question of freedom on the basis of predestination: "Since everything that happens takes place necessarily according to divine predestination, there is no freedom of the will." (*Ibid., Loci*, p. 10, lines 11 f.) Melanchthon was convinced of the scriptural basis of predestination, but he never really adopted it as an integral part of his own theology. Indeed, sharing the Humanist distrust for all traces of Stoic determinism, he prefers not "to imbue the minds of young people with the notion that everything happens, not by human intentions or endeavors, but by the will of God." (*Ibid.*, p. 12, lines 3 f.)

29. From the *Baccalaureate Theses* of September, 1519, Thesis 3: "Both divine law and natural law have decreed that God must be loved for his own sake." *Selected Writings* p. 17. In the Matthew lectures, p. 164, lines 26 f., and the *Loci*, p. 42, lines 28 f.

30. *Loci,* p. 42, lines 38 f.

31. *Ibid.,* p. 38, lines 32 f.

32. *Ibid.,* p. 46, lines 26 f.

33. *Baccalaureate Theses* 1-6, p. 17

34. CR XIV, 1048 f. Melanchthon's *Annotations* to John are found in CR XIV, 1047 f.

35. *Ibid.,* 1177 f.

36. *Ibid.,* 1173.

37. *Ibid.,* 1129.

38. *Ibid.,* 1129.

39. *Ibid.,* 1048 f.

40. *Ibid.,* 1115.

41. *Ibid.,* 1076. Cf. 1054, 1067, 1071, 1108, 1136, 1156, 1164, etc.

42. *Ibid.,* 1160. Cf. 1064, 1071, 1086, 1093, 1100, 1105, 1108, 1155, 1167, etc.

43. *Ibid.,* 1049. Cf. 1130, 1160, 1161, 1175, 1190, 1203.

44. Walter von Loewenich, *Luther und das Johanneische Christentum,* Munich: Chr. Kaiser Verlag, 1935, pp. 42 f. Cf. von Loewenich's *Luthers Theologia Crucis.* Munich: Chr. Kaiser Verlag, 1954, pp. 14 f. Melanchthon did not use the specific term *theologia crucis,* a term which Luther used in contrast to the Scholastics' *theologia gloriae,* which defined God not by the cross but in philosophical and theological speculation over God's heavenly, majestic attributes. Luther developed the idea more comprehensively than Melanchthon, as for example in terms of *deus absconditus* and *revelatus* ("God hidden and revealed"). But concerning the cross as God's revelation, Luther and Melanchthon are in basic agreeemnt.

45. Cf. *John,* CR XIV. 1054, 1061, 1065, 1102, 1126, 1152, 1154, 1157, 1178, 1188, 1196.

46. Bretschneider, for example, writes in his introduction to the *Annotations,* "For Melanchthon everywhere defends Luther's opinion concerning the bondage of the will and disputes Erasmus' teaching of the free will. For this reason Luther recommends the book." CR XIV, 1043 f.

47. *Matthew,* p. 164, lines 19 f. Cf. 135, 9 f.: *Loci,* 41, 34 f.

48. *Matthew,* p. 164, lines 26 f.

49. *Loci,* p. 42, lines 28 f.

50. *Ibid.,* p. 41, lines 28 f.

51. "For since they are called 'natural,' their formulas ought to be collected by a method of human reason through a syllogism. That is precisely what I have not yet seen done by anyone, and I hardly know whether it can be done at all, since our human nature is so enslaved and blinded." *Ibid.,* p. 41, lines 23 f.

52. "Since God commands us to love him above all else, it does not follow that it is in our power to do so just because it is demanded.

Indeed, simply because he commands us, it is not in our power."
Ibid., p. 36, lines 23 f.

53. "Natural and divine law order man to do that which the power of human nature is incapable of doing. . . . Nor can the law bring us to do those things which satisfy this debt." *Matthew*, p. 135, lines 11 f. Cf. p. 150, lines 9 f.

54. *Bacc. Theses*, p. 17.

55. For example, he speaks of "human laws" over against divine laws: "Human laws command only certain external works, but divine laws are concerned with the Spirit." *Matthew*, p. 150, lines 4 f. But "human" would likely refer here to "man-made" rather than natural or universal laws.

56. *Ibid.*, p. 135, lines 19 f., 23 f.

57. *Bacc. Theses*, p. 17. "God is hated as a legislator, so that finally we flee from God." Matthew, p. 135, lines 24 f.

58. *Paul and the Scholastics*, p. 36.

59. *Matthew*, p. 186, lines 6 f.

60. *Ibid.*, p. 138, lines 29 f.; 149, 5 f. Cf. 135, 22 ff.; 197, 31 f.; 147, 14 f.; 186, 21 f.; 149, 5 f.; *Paul and the Scholastics*, p. 36; *Theologica Institutio*, CR XXI, 54-X, 56-XIII.

61. *Matthew*, p. 147, lines 7 f.

62. *Paul and the Scholastics*, p. 34, 36.

63. *Matthew*, p. 136, lines 25 f. Prof. Stupperich writes also about Erasmus: "Erasmus was fond of describing God's will for salvation in the fashion of the ancient church: God's Son became man in order to make man like God." *Der Humanismus und die Wiedervereinigung der Konfessionen* (Leipzig, 1936), p. 9.

64. Chrysostom's Matthew Homilies are found in *Migne Series Graeca* (MSG), vols. 57 & 58. For specific references to Chrysostom, cf. *Matthew*, p. 147, lines 29 f.; p. 178, line 22. Striking similarities in other passages suggest that Melanchthon consulted Chrysostom on difficult verses as for example, Matt. 1:3 (139, 6 f.; MSG 57, 34 f.) and Matt. 10:16 (172, 27 f.; MSG 57, 390). Further parallels are too numerous to mention.

65. MSG 57, 26. Cf. *ibid.*, 25; also MSG 58, 780.

66. MSG 57, 199, 203, 206 f., 228, 229, 376; MSG 58, 480, 482, 698-700.

67. Indeed, the thesis by Bishop Gustav Aulen, *Christus Victor* (New York: Macmillan, 1958), holds that Luther's Christology is best reflected by this "classic" view. Actually, Bishop Aulen makes his case by overstating it. The fact of the matter is that in Luther's kaleidoscopic writings and utterances one can find ample evidences of practically all Christological types from the Bible and church history.

68. *Paul and the Scholastics*, p. 37. "For both peace of conscience and absolute virtue were unknown before the incarnation of Christ." *Ibid.*

69. *Matthew*, p. 147, lines 11 f. Cf. the summary, p. 149, lines 5 f.
"So Christ, who is both example and author of living, permits him-

self to be tempted in order that he might show us the marks of life in adversity. He gave himself to us that help might be ready at hand, as often as we call upon him in anxiety and difficulty." Ibid., p. 147, lines 7 f., 17 f.

70. It is not entirely correct to say that Melanchthon omits all references to Christ as a sacrifice. We find, for example, this statement: "Then Christ teaches that no one can come to the Father but through himself, for he himself is a sacrifice *(hostia)*, through whom we are reconciled to God." *Matthew*, p. 175, lines 10 f. But this sentence stands apart from the mainstream of Melanchthon's thought at this time. Furthermore, the phrase which follows, ". . . to God, through whom alone the Spirit of righteousness is given" (p. 175, lines 12 f.) suggests that the purpose of the sacrifice is in the context of the Humanist's ethical interest rather than the placating of the wrath of God.

71. "Christ bore this curse of the law, this judgment of the law." *Loci*, p. 127, lines 16 f.

72. Cf. Rolf Schäfer, *Christologie und Sittlichkeit in Melanchthons frühen Loci* (Tübingen: J.C.B. Mohr, Paul Siebeck, 1961). pp. 42-46, for a complete summary of Christological terms in the *Loci*.

73. Schäfer, *op. cit.*, pp. 28-30.

74. In this respect Schäfer is correct when he says that "apparently Melanchthon had no theological use for the reality of Christ as the reality of a human being." *Op. cit.*, p. 40.

75. *Loci*, p. 106, lines 12 f.

76. *Ibid.*, p. 106, lines 18 f. Thirdly, in the summary theses Christ is described as he "who placated the Father." *Ibid.*, p. 122, lines 34 f.

77. "The absurd consequences resulting from this conception of Melanchthon speak for themselves: When one asks how the sacrificial death of Christ could take place, the only answer can be that it is accomplished only through Christ. . . . The motivating initiative of God the Father . . . is completely lacking. Instead it is replaced by the initiative of Christ." *Ibid.*, p. 78, including fn. 1. Schäfer charges that "in the middle of this stands a teaching of satisfaction and sacrifice which is inadequately thought out." *Ibid.*, p. 77.

78. When Schäfer says, "It seems that Melanchthon never felt the impulse to formulate the idea of satisfaction more logically, in the footsteps of Anselm" (p. 79), he makes it clear how he has missed the real concern of Melanchthon.

There is, of course, much similarity between Anselm and Melanchthon. Indeed, any sacrificial Christology cannot help being similar to Anselm's teachings at one point or another. The clarity and simplicity of Anselm's arguments very likely also impressed Melanchthon. Prof. Maurer asserts that Melanchthon remains closely related to Anselm ("Zur Komposition der Loci Melanchthons von 1521," *Luther Jahrbuch*, Berlin: Lutherisches Verlagshaus, 1958, p. 169). But it is specifically Anselm's logical foundation which Melanchthon could not adopt, such as his ontological view of God, the founding of God's action in his "honor," the deemphasis of God's love, etc.

Cf. also the comments concerning Anselm below, ch. III, p. 98.

79. *Loci*, p. 106, lines 12 f. Cf. p. 6, lines 19 f.; p. 7, lines 16 f.

80. *Ibid.*, p. 95, lines 37 f.

81. *Ibid.*, p. 69, lines 27 f.; p. 68, lines 29 f.; p. 82, lines 31 f.

82. *Ibid.*, p. 68, line 28 f.

83. "Furthermore, the pledge of all these promises is Christ, whereby all promises in Scriptures are to be referred to him, promises which at first are obscure, then finally are clearly revealed." *Loci*, p. 67, lines 25 f. Cf. p. 124, lines 37 f.

84. "We have said that the Gospel is the promise of grace. Moreover, next to the promises are the signs. For in the Scriptures the signs are added to the promises as a seal, reminding us of the promises, and are certain testimonies of the divine will toward us." *Loci*, p. 141, lines 25 f. Cf. the section "On Signs," p. 140, lines 23 f.

85. "Some call them sacraments; we call them signs, or if you prefer, sacramental signs." *Ibid.*, p. 143, lines 29 f.

86. "Now Paul calls Christ himself a sacrament." *Ibid.*, p. 143, lines 31 f. Cf. in the Vulgate, Col. 1:27; 1 Tim. 3:16.

In this discussion of signs, promises and sacraments, one notes a marked similarity to Luther's *Babylonian Captivity* of 1520.

87. *Loci*, p. 117, lines 20 f.; Cf. 101, 30 f.; 124, 33 f.

88. John 14:9. CR XIV, 1170, 1172, 1188, 1199.

"The Son is the embodiment of the thought and purpose of the Father, whose will cannot be known except in the Son. . . . All knowledge of the Father comes from the Son. Therefore no one knows the Father unless through the Word and in the Word, which is the Son." *Ibid.*, 1066 ("Filius sententia patris est . . ."). Cf. 1053, 1119, 1137, 1179.

89. *Ibid.*, 1172, 1119, 1102 f.

90. *Ibid.*, 1050. In addition to John's term "word" (logos) Melanchthon also refers to Col. 1:15, "He is the image. . . ."

91. Melanchthon adds that the Holy Spirit is a "force" or "agitation" (agitatio). He completes his sketch of the Trinity by speaking of all three: "One cannot separate the actions of the three. The Father is the one from which all action originates. The Son is the means by which this action is done (consilium agendi). And the Holy Spirit is the force or agitation itself" (John, 1050).

Melanchthon's stress on the divinity of Christ, establishing the validity of his work, has thus led him inevitably to an analysis of Trinitarian doctrine, which he had tried to avoid in the *Loci*. It is a significant step and charts the way for his own future as well as the future of "orthodox" Lutheran theology. See below, chapter 3.

92. *Ibid.*, 1047.

93. *Ibid.*, 1117. "Because John begins with the divinity of Christ, our faith should be aroused, so that we believe without doubting that the

will of God is to remit sins, because Christ, who himself is God, proclaims the forgiveness of sins." *Ibid.*, 1051. Cf. 1047, 1048, 1096.

94. *Ibid.*, 1051 f. Arius' view, that Jesus was not by his very substance equal to the Father, was condemned at the Nicene Council in 325 B.C. Melanchthon's criticism of Arius is an implicit rejection of all "Antiochean" Christology, which stresses particularly strongly Christ's human nature. This fact is noteworthy, considering both Melanchthon's leaning toward Greek "Alexandrian" trend, which plays a strong role in his (and Luther's) later works.

In his exegesis of John's Gospel Luther also emphasizes Christ's divinity. Philip Watson writes, "Luther's entire theology can be said to stand or fall with the divinity of Christ." *Let God Be God* (Philadelphia: Muhlenberg Press, 1949), p. 102. (Cf. all of Ch. 13, "The Incarnated Deity.")

Cf. also von Loewenich, *Luther und das joh. Christentum*, pp. 20 f., pp. 38 f.; Eduard Ellwein, "Die Christusverkündigung in Luthers Auslegung des Johannesevangeliums," in *Kerygma und Dogma*, 1960, pp. 31 f.; also Luther's sermon in 1522 on John's Prologue, WA 10/I/1, 184, 19 f.; 191, 7 f.

95. *John*, 1115.

96. "When the figure of the serpent was lifted up, it meant that the figure of sin was elevated, that is, Christ, who became sin for us. The dead represents the death of sin." *John*, 1081. This image—the serpent on the cross—Melanchthon took for his own crest, or seal.

97. *Ibid.*, 1071.

98. *Ibid.*, 1048, 1065, 1071, 1077, 1104, 1133, 1145, 1164, 1179, etc.

99. *Ibid.*, 1080.

100. *Ibid.*, 1056, 1057, 1072, 1117.

101. *Ibid.*, 1090. Cf. 1062, 1066, 1071, 1074, 1096, 1102, 1112, 1160, 1161, 1176, 1180.

102. *Ibid.*, 1158.

103. *Ibid.*

104. "The discussion between Christ and Peter indicates the meaning of Christ's washing the disciples' feet." *Ibid.*, 1160.

105. *Ibid.*

106. "In sum, this washing and submission of Christ represents the fruit which thereby comes to us, for whom he has come as a servant." *Ibid.*, 1163.

107. Though the terms "grace" and "faith" were of course defined differently by the Humanists, this similarity in outlook was in fact a basis for later, though abortive, attempts at Roman Catholic-Protestant reconciliation. Cf. Prof. Stupperich, *Der Humanismus und die Wiedervereinigung, op. cit.*, pp. 113 f.

108. Cf. Prof. Maurer, *"Lex Spiritualis* bei Melanchthon bis 1521." *Melanchthon-Studien*, pp. 105-108; StA IV, pp. 157 f.

109. *Matthew*, StA IV, p. 148, lines 31 f.

110. *Ibid.*, p. 206, lines 9 f. "It is necessary that we are born again in the family line of Jesus. How? Through faith." *Ibid.*, p. 137, lines 16 f.

111. *Fiducia:* Matthew, p. 164, line 11; 166, 23; 170, 10; 185, 2. *Confidens* or *Confidentia:* p. 136, 13, 17; 184, 35; 204, 22; 206, 10 f.
   In Luther's *Operationes in Psalmos* the idea of faith as trust *(fiducia)* is also prominent: WA V p. 91, line 28; 93, 42; 94, 25, 39; 95, 16; 109, 31; 111, 16; 117, 22, 118, 15, 19, 36; 160, 32; 168, 27; 294, 38.

112. *Matthew,* StA IV, p. 177, lines 17 f.; 186, 1 f; 206, 15 f. Melanchthon also refers to the Word as the "beginning of justification," p. 177, line 26; 179, 14. Cf. 178, 26.

113. *Ibid.*, p. 196, lines 13 f. Also 190, 5 f.: Christ "calls us back from the feelings of the flesh *(sensus carnis)* to the Spirit."
   This *raptus* concept occurs also in the *Theologica Institutio,* and its use is noteworthy because one sees how Melanchthon is already moving from a Humanist to a Pauline understanding of man. In the Matthew lectures it is used within the implied Platonic framework of a flesh-spirit or earthly-heavenly dualism. We are enraptured mainly "from the flesh" to "heavenly" or "spiritual" things. In the *Institutio,* which is a preliminary study of Paul's epistle to the Romans, the distinction shifts to good and evil, in terms of God's law. As sinner, man is enraptured into "evil" or "depravity" (CR XXI, 51-IV, 53-VII, VIII), but the Christian is enraptured to the "good" *(Ibid.,* 51, 52-IV, 54-VIII, 55-XIII). This small difference is one of the steps that led to the "Reformation" anthropology of the *Loci.*

114. *Matthew,* p. 148, lines 28 f. Cf. 154, 2 f.: "Christ is the 'end of the law,' as Paul says because he gives the Spirit for doing the law and is a sacrifice for our sins." Also 153, 32; 176, 27 f.

115. Cf. the *Theologica Institutio,* where the Spirit is described as "justifier" and "purifier." CR XXI, 56-XIII.

116. "Righteousness is not simulated or pretended, but is something actual and substantial, superior to the affections of the flesh." *Matthew,* p. 179, lines 29 f. Cf. 150, 8 f.; 154, 12 f.; in the Institutio, CR XXI, 54-X, 55-XIII, 56.

117. *Matthew,* p. 176, lines 27 f.

118. Actually one sees traces of both Humanist and Reformer in these lectures, in statements that can be interpreted one way or another. Melanchthon speaks as a Humanist: "Furthermore, our justification is nothing other than the mortification of our flesh and our affections." Matthew, p. 173, lines 5 f. As a Reformer he writes: "Righteousness of faith is surely the soul trusting in Christ." *Ibid.,* 177, 11.

119. Cf. Prof. Robert Stupperich, *Der Unbekannte Melanchthon* (Stuttgart: Kohlhammer Verlag, 1961), pp. 14, 131 f., and also the suggestions of K. Meissinger, that Melanchthon wrote both the Foreword and the Epilogue to Luther's commentary, WA II, 57, XVI f. The English translation of the commentary is found in *Luther's Works—American Edition,* Vol. XXVII.

120. *Luther's Works,* XXVII, p. 231.

121. *Ibid.*, 241 f., 270.

122. *Ibid.*, 223 f. Cf. *ibid.*, 229. Therefore our works are not primarily "works of the Law . . . they are works of love. Nor are they done on account of the Law, which commands; they are done on account of the brother, who wants or needs them. . . ." *Ibid.*, 329. In his 1519 sermon on "Two Kinds of Righteousness," Luther compares the "alien righteousness, that is the righteousness of another (Christ's) instilled from without," with "our proper righteousness, not because we alone work it, but because we work with that first and alien righteousness." *Luther's Works* XXXI. 297, 299.

123. *Luther's Works*, XXVII, p. 231.

124. *Ibid.*, p. 227.

125. *Loci*, StA II, p. 88, lines 8 f.

126. *Ibid.*, p. 108, line 21.

127. *Ibid.*, p. 131, lines 35 f.

128. *Ibid.*, p. 108, lines 20 f. "Flesh" in the *Loci* refers to the *whole* man. Cf. *ibid.*, 108, 25 f.; p. 48, lines 25 f.

129. *Ibid.*, p. 130, lines 31 f.

130. *Ibid.*, p. 130, lines 30 f.

131. This section includes *ibid.*, p. 130, line 23 to p. 132, line 13.

132. *Ibid.*, p. 132, line 10.

133. Otto Ritschl claimed that "Melanchthon's earlier, 'realistic' concept of justification" is reflected in the passage, ". . . the Spirit is the very justification of the heart" *(Ibid.*, 133, 2 f). "Die Entwicklung der Rechtfertigungslehre Melanchthons bis zum Jahre 1527," *Theologische Studien und Kritiken*, 1912, pp. 528 f. But the context of this *Loci* passage is not referring to the ethical aspect of the Spirit's work. Rather it means that the justified person is now a "spiritual," not carnal, man *(Ibid.*, 132, 34 f.; 133, 7, 11). Melanchthon merely intends to say that the spiritual man is justified, an idea general enough to apply either to Humanist or to Reformer.

134. *Loci*, 47, 37 f.

135. *Ibid.*, 86, 15, 23 f.; 87, 1 f. The progression of Melanchthon's thought can be traced in the two preliminary studies of the *Loci*. In the *Institutio* we find the earlier conception: "Grace, which Paul also terms the Spirit, is that by which we are illuminated, purged, and driven to the good." CR XXI, 53-VIII. Cf. 54-VIII. In the *Rerum Theologicarum Capita*, written very likely about a year later, in 1520, we read: "Grace actually means *favor*" (CR XXI, 36).

136. ". . . so the Gospel is the promise of the grace or mercy of God, that is, the forgiveness of sins and the testimony of God's benevolence." *Loci*, StA II, 67, 19 f.

137. "In sum, grace is nothing other than the forgiveness or remission of sins." *Ibid.*, 87, 24 f. Otto Ritschl pointed out that Melanchthon does not actually identify justification and forgiveness. *Op. cit.*, p. 528. This is correct, but Melanchthon has laid the foundation which will lead

him unavoidably in that direction. His teaching in the *Loci* is not so "relatively yet undeveloped" as Ritschl claimed.

138. *Loci*, StA II, 88, 35 f.; 92, 25 f.

139. *Ibid.*, 93, 38 f.; 109, 1 f. If salvation were from works, Melanchthon says, the conscience would never be at rest. *Ibid.*, 117, 29 f.

140. *Ibid.*, 107, 32 f. Cf. 30, 3 f; 92, 24; 96, 34 f.; 107, 23 f.; 116, 11 f.; 132, 10 f.; 141, 9; 158, 3 f.

141. *Ibid.*, 157, 38 f. Cf. 88, 18 f.; 139, 1 f; 157, 38 f.

142. One notable exception is from Melanchthon's *Baccalaureate Theses,* No. 10: "All of our righteousness is a gracious imputation of God" (Omnis justitia nostra est gratuita dei imputatio, *Selected Writings,* p. 17). Insofar as this use of *imputatio* is entirely without explanation or elaboration from Melanchthon's other writings of this time, it can hardly be characterized as an integral part of Melanchthon's early theology. Adolf Sperl's conclusion seems most likely: Baccalaureate theses at that time did not represent firmly held convictions, but were proposed to stimulate debate and discussion on provocative topics. *Melanchthon zwischen Humanismus und Reformation* (Munich: Chr. Kaiser Verlag, 1959), p. 110 fn. 59. The thesis does, however, suggest the direction Melanchthon's thinking is moving.

143. But both Melanchthon and Luther borrowed the negative usage from the Scholastics. Our remaining sins are *non imputantur,* "not imputed," but are forgiven. Melanchthon: *Matthew,* 154, 12 f.; 176, 27 f.; CR XXI, 57; *Loci,* 108, 35 f. Luther uses *non imputantur* to explain the formulae *simul iustus et peccator* and *nondum plene in re sed in spe,* answering the question, "How are sinners justified in Christ though they are still sinners?" Luther's Works XXVII, 227, 231.

144. "Thus it comes about that just as all became sinners because of another's sin, so by Another's righteousness all become righteous. . . ." *Ibid.*, 222. Cf. also above, p. 150, fn. 122.

145. *Loci* p. 88, lines 23 f. Cf. 101, 5 f. Genesis 15:6 and Romans 4:5 are translated by Melanchthon with *reputare,* 88, 25 f.; 115, 18 f.

146. *Ibid.*, 88, 8 f., 18 f.

147. "For this is liberty, that all right of the law to accuse and condemn us has been done away with." *Ibid.*, 127, 9 f.

148. *Ibid.*, 126, 16 f.

149. *Ibid.*, 127, 4 f.

150. *Ibid.*, 128, 28 f.

151. *Ibid.*, 128, 26 f. Cf. 133, 16 f.

152. *Ibid.*, 129, 19 f.

153. *Ibid.*, 130, 23 f.

154. *Ibid.*, 130, 25 f.

155. This is the thesis of Schäfer, that the seeds of the *tertius usus legis* are found in this first *Loci* edition. In this he is correct. Cf. also below, chapter III, pp. 119 f.

156. *Loci.*, 38, 17; 128, 24, 26; 129, 36; 133, 34; 135, 12; 136, 8, 34.

157. *John*, 1086. Also 1066: "Therefore, because the truth is our justification, the truth is the knowledge of God, and all knowledge of the Father is the Son. . . . Justification is nothing but the knowledge of God."

158. *Ibid.*, 1062.

159. *Ibid.*, 1197. Cf. 1059, 1069, 1108, 1122, 1125, 1135, 1156, 1195.

160. *Ibid.*, 1080.

161. *Ibid.*, 1080, 1082.

162. *Ibid.*, 1066.

163. *Ibid.*, 1079.

164. "For this reason Christ's flesh was manifest to all, that we might believe in Christ crucified, which means to know that we too must be mortified, and believe that life is received through death." *John*, 1104. Cf. 1049, 1092, 1100, 1105, 1130, 1154, 1159, 1164, 1176, 1191. In the *Loci* Melanchthon spoke of our mortification, but it was related to repentance rather than an ethical following of Christ.

165. *John*, 1188.

166. *Ibid.*, 1151. This is another argument against the freedom of the will, Melanchthon says, since the natural man would never do this on his own volition.

167. *Ibid.*, 1103, 1134, 1149, 1152, 1174. The fact that Melanchthon terms the Christian life one of afflictions is likely due to historical reasons as well as theological. In Humanist optimism he had naively expected a surging renewal of enlightenment and piety following the restoration of biblical truth. Instead, he was confronted by the rabble and chaos of the "enthusiasts" during Luther's stay at the Wartburg (1521-1522). His disillusionment convinced him that the Reformation Church faced many afflictions in its path.

168. *Ibid.*, 1163.

169. *Ibid.*, 1108.

170. *Ibid.*, 1062.

171. *Oportet enim nos similes fieri imaginis Christi*, 1049, 1050, 1107, 1136, 1159, 1170, 1176, 1191.

172. Bernhard Lohse, "Luthers Christologie im Ablassstreit," *Luther-Jahrbuch* (Berlin: Lutherisches Verlagshaus, 1960), p. 58. Cf. p. 57, 60. Cf. von Loewenich, *Theologia Crucis, op. cit.*, pp. 157 f., 164 f. Cf. also the chapter "Theologia Crucis" in Ernst Bizer's *Theologie der Verheissung, Studien zur Theologie des jungen Melanchthon* (Neukirchen: Neukirchner Verlag, 1964), pp. 253 f., 258 f.

173. Lohse, *op. cit.*, p. 56. Lohse interprets Luther: "As Christ hung on the cross . . . so also must the Christian be crucified." Cf. also von Loewenich's chapter, "Das Leben unter dem Kreuz," *op. cit.*, pp. 148 f., especially p. 160. Von Loewenich terms Luther's concept "crucified with Christ" *(concrucifigi Christo)*, p. 15, 149.

174. *Luther's Works* XXVII, 308. Johannes von Walter wrote about Luther: "One thing is certain—as Christ's path to glory was through the cross,

so this should be the path also of the Christian." "Luthers Christus-bild," *Luther-Jahrbuch* (Weimar: Verlag Hermann Böhlaus, 1939), p. 20.

175. These *Anfechtungen* are not limited in the narrow sense to Luther's pre-Reformation agonized search for a gracious God, but refer to the broader definition: Christian life in a hostile, difficult, problem-ridden world *(das angefochtene Leben).*

176. Von Loewenich, *Theologia Crucis,* p. 163.

177. Von Loewenich, *Luther und das joh. Christentum,* p. 47.

178. So also Erasmus: "Erasmus looks to the moral example which Christ furnishes." W. Maurer, *op. cit.,* p. 158.

179. Erich Seeberg summarized Luther's views: "What happens with Christ happens also to us. . . . This presupposes the conviction that Christ and we are one together." *Christus: Wirklichkeit und Urbild* (Stuttgart: Kohlhammer Verlag, 1937), p. 7, 11. Cf. also Luther's *Operationes in Psalmos,* WA 5, 158, 18 f. Cf. below, Luther and Melanchthon's letter to Brenz, at the close of Ch. II.

180. Cf. Bizer's section on "Melanchthon und Luther" in the chapter on the *Annotations to John, op. cit.,* pp. 272 f.

181. Adolf Sperl notes "how little Melanchthon is concerned with 'eternal' salvation," *op. cit.,* p. 125.

182. Again, Erasmus furnishes the best example of this.

183. *Loci,* p. 144, lines 22 f.

184. *Ibid.,* p. 143, lines 24.

185. *Ibid.,* p. 143, lines 30 f.

186. *Ibid.,* p. 145, lines 17 f.

187. *Ibid.,* p. 156, lines 26 f. Cf. also Melanchthon's 1521 theses concerning signs and sacraments in his "Propositions on the Mass," *Selected Writings,* p. 63 f.

Chapter II. SPOKESMAN

188. *Epitome renovatae ecclesiasticae doctrinae,* CR I, 703 f.; in English as *Summary of Doctrine, Selected Writings,* pp. 93 f.

189. CR XXVI, 7 f. German version: "Instructions for Visitors Examiners to Pastors in Electoral Saxony," CR XXVI, 49.

190. CR XXVI, 161 f. Cf. also J. L. Neve, *Introduction to the Symbolical Books of the Lutheran Church* (Columbus, 1956), pp. 86 f.

191. CR XXVI, 129 f. Cf. Neve, *op. cit.,* pp. 88 f.

192. Letter to Bugenhagen, July 5, 1537, WA *Briefe* VIII, 96.

193. We shall see, however, that Melanchthon will have to concern himself with the incarnation in later years, not in the specific context of justification, but as a foundation for justification in response to the radical anti-trinitarians.

194. Quoted from the translation of Prof. Wilhelm Pauck in his superlative article "Luther and Melanchthon," in *Luther and Melanchthon*, Vilmos Vajta, ed. (Philadelphia: Fortress Press, 1961), p. 22.

195. Prof. Pauck comments, "What Melanchthon sought to make clear by doctrinal definitions, Luther explained by pointing to the actuality of the believer's communion with Christ. Here lay the deepest difference between them." However, Prof. Pauck's conclusion, that "Melanchthon gave to Luther's understanding of the Gospel a humanistic-scientific form which . . . was foreign to Luther's spiritual outlook," is too strongly worded. Had Melanchthon's interpretation been so "foreign" to Luther, doubtless the Reformer would have taken steps to set the matter right.

Chapter III. THEOLOGIAN

196. WA XX, 345, 6 f. Paul Wilhelm Gennrich writes, in his dissertation "Die Cristologie Luthers in Abendmahlsstreit," that "the whole significance of Christ as mediator between God and man lies for Luther in the complete unity of the two natures in Christ" (Königsberg: Otto Kummel Druckerei, 1929), p. 61.

197. This term *communicatio idiomatum* literally means "the sharing, participation, or communion of the characteristics." It refers to the characteristics of each of the natures of Christ sharing in the person of Christ. This concept plays a large part in Reformation Christology, particularly in the precise understanding of the Lord's Supper.

198. WA XX, 345, 21 f.

199. WA XVIII, 186, 38 f., *Luther's Works* XL, 197.

Prof. Gustav Plitt wrote, "Of course Karlstadt had not exactly resurrected the ancient Christological heresies, but Luther recognized very clearly the bases of his opponent's theological outlook, namely that Karlstadt's doctrine of the Sacrament would logically distort the doctrine of Christ." *Einleitung in die Augustana* (Erlangen, 1868), p. 87.

For a helpful, contemporary viewpoint, cf. Robert H. Fischer's article "Luther's Stake in the Lord's Supper Controversy," in *Dialog*, Winter, 1963, pp. 50 f.

200. WA XXIII, 201, 31 f., LW XXXVII, 99.

201. *Ibid.*, 143, 30 f., LW XXXVII, 63 f.

202. WA XXVI, 326, 29 f., LW XXXVII, 214.

203. Luther had not yet worked out his concept of the *communicatio idiomatum*, but it is clear that in this controversy he had laid the foundation for his later thinking.

204. WA *Briefe* III, 433, 8 f.; WA XVIII, 547, fn. 2. Cf. also the letter to Lazarus Spengler from the same day, WA *Briefe* III, 432, 1 f.

205. Melanchthon writes, for example, "Here it isn't enough to learn that Christ is God and man, or by what means his natures could have been joined together. . . . Much more to be considered is why he

who is proclaimed as the remission of sins must be God." *John,* CR XIV, 1047.

206. CR I, 760, Cf. also Melanchthon's "Concerning Karlstadt's Opinion of the Lord's Supper" of 1529. CR I, 1036.

207. CR I, 911.

208. CR I, 949.

209. CR I, 1049.

210. In the spring of 1530 Melanchthon published a document quoting church fathers to prove that the Lutheran teaching stems from the ancient church. CR XXIII, 733 f.

211. In view of Melanchthon's later teachings concerning the Eucharist, Adolf Sperl and Otto Ritschl both date the beginnings of Melanchthon's particular ideas from this period of 1530-1531, following the reception of Oecolampadius' *Dialogus.* Sperl, *op. cit.,* p. 173, and Ritschl, *Dogmengeschichte des Protestantismus,* Vol. I (Leipzig, 1908), p. 280, fn. 1.

212. From the Latin text, which was Melanchthon's "working language" at Augsburg and is perhaps academically the more "official" version. However, a comparison of the Latin and German texts continues to be a subject of discussion. Some scholars have felt that the German text is more "Lutheran," since the inclusion of the words "under the form of bread and wine" echo Luther's own words in the Small Catechism, Article 6, "under the bread and wine." But there is no evidence that Luther detected any significant difference in the two versions.

213. CR II, 225 f.

214. CR II, 226.

215. CR II, 224.

216. *Inclusio localis,* CR II, 224.

217. CR II, 222. Cf. in Ch. IV, pp. 132 f.

218. CR I, 1048, 1050.

219. Letter to Nikolaus Gerbel in the spring of 1528, CR I, 974. Cf. CR I, 899.

220. "Ten Questions Concerning Melanchthon, the Fathers, and the Eucharist," in *Luther and Melanchthon, op. cit.* pp. 147 f.

221. CR II, 787. Cf. Melanchthon's letter to Bucer during the Diet at Augsburg, CR II, 222, and his letter to Schwebel from April, 1529, CR I, 1047.

222. Cf. Robert Stupperich, "Melanchthon und die Taufer." *Kirche und Dogma,* 1957, pp. 154-158 and Fraenkel, *Testimonium Patrum* (Geneva: E. Droz. 1961), p. 46, fn. 192. Also Melanchthon's letters to Duke John, CR I, 1099, and to Duke Henry of Saxony, CR I, 1103.

223. CR I, 1084.

224. Article 1 of the Augsburg Confession rejects the "Samosatenes, old *and new.*" To this, Theodore Tappert notes, "Followers of Paul of Samosata, who taught in the third century that Jesus was a man specially endowed by the Spirit. The 'new Samosatenes' were anti-

Trinitarian spiritualists of the sixteenth century. . . ." *(The Book of Concord.* Theodore Tappert, ed. Philadelphia: Fortress Press, 1959), p. 28.

225. CR II, 630. Also: "Servetus imagines that Christ is not truly the natural and begotten Son of God. . . . This is the main point and heart of these controversies." CR II, 661.

226. *Ibid.*

227. CR. XXI, 351.
The Loci edition of 1535 is found in CR XXI, 334 f. Melanchthon's third version of the *Loci* appeared first in 1543-1544. He continued making various smaller changes and additions in numerous printings of this third edition, up until the last printing in his lifetime, in 1559. This last printing of 1559 is found in CR XXI, 601 f. and StA II, 165 f. Prof. Clyde Manschreck has provided us with an English translation of Melanchthon's own 1555 German translation from the Latin edition in *Melanchthon on Christian Doctrine.* New York: Oxford University Press, 1965.

228. Melanchthon writes, "This method does not proceed a priori, that is, from the unknown being of God to the recognition of his will, but from the knowledge of Christ and the therein offered grace in the gospel to the recognition of God's presence." CR XXI, 352.
With this statement Melanchthon is agreeing with Luther's concept of *deus absconditus* and *deus revelatus* ("God hidden and revealed") although he does not use Luther's terms.

229. CR XXI, 352.

230. *Ibid.,* 354.

231. From Melanchthon's *Explicatio* of the Nicene Creed, CR XXIII, 381.

232. CR XXI, 354. Cf. the latest *Loci* edition, published in 1559, StA II, p. 178, 10 f. 184, 2 f. and in the *Explicatio,* CR XXIII, 360, 501. These last two works contain perhaps Melanchthon's most detailed presentation of the Trinity. (The 1559 *Loci* will henceforth be quoted with page and line numbers from StA II.)

233. CR XXI, 354.

234. *Ibid.* Cf. 1559 *Loci,* 183, 2 f.

235. CR XXI, 355.

236. CR XXIII, 381.

237. 1559 *Loci,* 204, 32 f.

238. "Opera Trinitatis ad extra sunt indivisa."
From the *Examen Ordinandorum* of 1554, CR XXIII, 7. Cf. StA VI, 272, 22 f.; CR VIII, 667; CR XXIII, 374, 384, 511; CR XXIV, 578.

239. "It is easier to refute the Arians, for if one concedes that the Logos is a person—which the Arians confess—then John clearly testifies that the Logos is God." CR XXI, 358.

240. 1559 *Loci,* 193, 19 f.

241. Paul of Samosata was the able bishop of Antioch from c. 260-272 A.D., who was the chief proponent of "Dynamic Monarchianism," the view

that the Logos was merely an attribute of the Father, which inspired and dwelt in Jesus. Thereby Jesus did not have the same substance with God.

242. In contrast with the "Antiochene" school, which tended to begin with Jesus, who then was filled or indwelt with the Spirit, or Logos— although such brief summaries are bound to oversimplify.

It should be noted that Luther too was far more "Alexandrian" than "Antiochene," even though he is a bit more difficult to classify than Philip.

243. In contrast, saying almost nothing about the extreme Alexandrian deviations—Apollinaris, Eutyches, the Monophysites and Monothelites, etc.

244. From the *Explicatio,* CR XXIII, 369. Cf. 1559 *Loci,* 201, 17 f.

245. CR XXIII, 5.

246. *Examen,* CR XXIII, 5. Cf. CR XXIII, 368 f.; StA VI, 265, 11 f.; CR VIII, 638 f.

247. Apparently he disregarded, as did the Alexandrians, the danger that this tends to reduce the human nature to an inert substance with the Logos taking over the role of mind or spirit. Indeed, Melanchthon even says, "The Logos assumes human nature and gives life to this mass *(massa),* restoring life to its members"! StA VI, 226, 37 f. Cf. CR XXIII, 5.

This whole Alexandrian trend was adopted in turn by the Lutheran theologians of the 17th century.

248. *Examen,* CR XXIII, 6. Cf. CR XXIII, 508.

249. 1559 *Loci,* 200, 1 f.

250. StA VI, 265, 10 f.; CR XXIII, 371, 505, 509.

251. StA VI, 262, 34 f. Cf. 1559 *Loci,* 198, 11 f.
"Christ was wounded, God was wounded, God died. . . . These statements are true by the *communicatio idiomatum.*" CR XXIII, 6. Cf. CR VII, 1145; XXIII, 509.

252. StA VI, 267, 10 f. Cf. CR XXIII, 6, 373. This concept was particularly emphasized after Osiander had taught that Christ's divine nature justifies us and was opposed by Stancarus, who said that Christ is mediator according to his human nature.

253. 1559 *Loci,* 199, 3 f. Melanchthon works out a strong critique of Arius and Nestorius on the basis of the *communicatio idiomatum.* Cf. CR XXIII, 371, 374 f., 376 f. 200, 27 f.; 371, 37 f.; StA VI, 262, 4 f.

254. The opening definition in the *Formula of Concord* is precisely that taught by Melanchthon: ". . . therefore any property, though it belongs only to one of the natures, is ascribed not only to the respective nature as something separate but to the entire person who is simultaneously God and man (whether he is called God or whether he is called man)." *Formula of Concord (Solid Declaration),* Article 8, Para. 36, Tappert, ed., *op cit.,* p. 598.

255. Cf. *Book of Concord,* Tappert ed., p. 598, fn. 6.

256. Augsburg Confession, Article 2, p. 29.

257. *Apology*, Article 2, Paragraph 7, p. 101. Melanchthon continues ". . . in their awkward way they ask whether it came through contact with the apple or through the serpent's breath, and whether medicine can cure it."

258. *Ibid.*

259. *Ibid.*, para. 15, p. 102.

260. *Ibid.*, para. 16, p. 102.

261. Melanchthon strikes a telling blow by quoting Peter Lombard—"Peter Lombard is not afraid to say that original righteousness is the very likeness of God which he put into man"—a reference which must have caused the *Confutation* authors to wince! *Ibid.;* para. 21 p. 103.

    Actually this reflects Luther's comments on the First Commandment in the *Large Catechism,* where Luther derives his concept of righteousness and sin also in terms of man's relationship to God.

262. *Ibid.*, para. 25, p. 103. "Since nature in its weakness cannot fear and love God or believe in him, it seeks and loves carnal things; either it despises the judgment of God in its security, or it hates him in its terror." *Ibid.*, para. 24, 103.

    "Concupiscence" is also defined as "lust," man's twisted desires.

263. *Ibid.*, para. 26, p. 103.

264. *Ibid.*, para. 3, p. 101.

265. 1550 *Loci*, 220, 22 f.

266. As we noted in the first chapter, it was his mistrust of determinism which caused him to be uneasy about the doctrine of predestination. He accepted predestination of course as a scriptural truth, but made it clear that it was not the same as fatalism. Predestination should not be an independent part of discussion or speculation, but a part of the Gospel. "Ultimately the cause of predestination is none other than justification" *(Loci* 1535, CR XXI, 450). God's promise is universal to all men, not limited by predestination (CR XV, 505). One should neither give up in apathy because everything is determined, nor worry about being elected, but trust in God's promises.

    This fear of determinism and fatalism also caused Philip to take great pains in rejecting any thought of contingency—that God caused sin—from Article 19 in the *Confession* to the lengthy section in the last *Loci* edition of 1559, "De causa peccati et de contingentia," 1559 *Loci*, 224-236.

267. Article 18, para. 1, p. 39.

268. *Ibid.*, para. 2, 3, p. 39.

269. Cf. the last *Loci*, StA II, 238, 7-28.

    Nevertheless, the question of man's will, specifically man's will in conversion, becomes a heated issue in Melanchthon's later years and during the decades between his death and the Formula of Concord. This particular problem, the "synergistic" controversy, will be dealt with in Chapter IV.

270. 1535 *Loci*, CR XXI, 405; 1559 *Loci, ibid.*, 321, 35 f. Cf. also the 1532 *Romans Commentary*, StA V, 97, 24 f.

271. 1535 *Loci* CR XXI, 405; 1559 *Loci,* StA II, 323, 21 f.; *Romans Com.,* StA V, 98, 6 f.

272. The "third use of the law," which has produced a flurry of discussion in recent years, will be examined in the section on Christian life.

273. CR XXIII, 579, cf. 1559 Loci, 255, 2 f.

274. CR XXIII, 573.

275. *Apology,* Article 4, para. 80, p. 118.

276. CR XV, 558. Cf. 1535 *Loci, ibid.,* 414: "The Gospel . . . contains the promise of Christ's benefits, which is the proper and chief doctrine of the Gospel. . . ."
    A few times Melanchthon uses the term "Gospel" to designate the whole Word of God, including the law. For example: "For the ministry of the Gospel is first to convict of sin . . ." (CR XV, 501), and in the 1535 *Loci,* 421: "The Gospel accuses of sin. . . ."

277. 1559 *Loci,* 783, 19 f. Cf. *Explicatio,* CR XXIII, 359, 360.

278. CR XXIII, 385.

279. *Ibid.*

280. *Ibid.*

281. Gospel of John 14:9. Cf. the exposition in the 1559 *Loci,* 174, 33 f.

282. CR VIII, 573.

283. CR XXIII, 23, 64.

284. 1559 *Loci,* 202, 5 f.; CR XXIII, 50.

285. CR XXIII, 74, 373; StA VI, 270, 3 f.; 274, 33.

286. 1559 *Loci,* 527, 4 f. Cf. CR XXIII, 68, 69, 74.

287. Both Reinhold Seeberg, *Lehrbuch der Dogmengeschichte,* Vol. 4 (Stuttgart: Benno Schwabe & Co., 1960), p. 468, and Peter Meinhold, *Melanchthon* (Berlin: Lutherisches Verlagshaus, 1960), p. 82, for example, point to Melanchthon's mention of Anselm, CR XXIV, 579, to persuade their readers that Philip based his views on Anselm.

288. StA VI, 272, 6 f. Cf. CR VIII, 532; 23, 73, 433, 465; *Apology,* Article 4, para. 291, p. 152.

289. CR XXIII, 511.

290. *Apology,* Articles 7 & 8, para. 5, p. 169.

291. CR XXIII, 443.

292. CR XXIII, 511.

293. *Apology,* Articles 7 & 8, para. 16, p. 171.

294. For example in the *Apology,* Article 16, para. 2, p. 222: "Christ's kingdom is spiritual; it is the knowledge of God in the heart, the fear of God and faith, the beginning of eternal righteousness and eternal life."

295. CR XXIII, 507. Cf. *ibid.,* 504.

296. CR IX, 409. Cf. CR XXIII, 503: "Christ was sent to collect the Church, to preserve the ministerium of the Gospel, and to be working through the reception of the Gospel. . . ."

297. Cf. CR I, 664, 684, 824, 829, 858, 953, etc.

298. Cf. CR I, 683, 686, 740, 741, 862, 869, 873, 888, 903, 913, 914, 918, 943, 951, 979, 981, 1000, 1003, 1017, 1060, 1093, etc.

299. *Scholia in epistolam Pauli ad Colossenses,* from 1527, StA IV, 278, 31 f.

300. *Apology,* Article 10, pp. 179 f.

301. CR I, 1049. It would be an unworthy thought, he continues, to think of Christ as "incarcerated" in heaven, and not totally among believers on earth.

302. Cf. *Scholia to Colossians, op. cit.,* 248, 9 f.; 283, 32 f.; *Visitation Articles* 12 & 18, CR XXVI, 20 f.

303. Prof. Robert Stupperich observes that for Luther "the incorporation or joining together of Christ in the believer is an essential element of the resulting justification. . . . In this context everything for Luther ultimately comes down to this union with (Gemeinschaft) Christ, to 'truly have Christ.'" "Die Rechtfertigungslehre bei Luther und Melanchthon." *Luther and Melanchthon, op. cit.,* p. 78.

304. *Augsburg Confession,* Article 4, p. 30.

305. Although the negative form—"sins not imputed"—was often borrowed from the Scholastics by both Luther and Melanchthon.

306. *Apology,* Article 4, para. 2, p. 107. The Roman Catholic arguments, on the other hand, obscure the glory and the benefits of Christ, and they rob pious consciences of the consolation offered them in Christ." *Ibid.,* para. 3, Cf. *ibid.,* para. 204, p. 135; para. 316-320, 324, pp. 156 f.; *Romans Com.* StA V, 102, 34 f.

307. *Apology,* Article 4, para. 48, p. 114.

308. *Confession,* Article 20, para. 23, p. 44.

309. StA V, 40, 7; 155, 16 f. Actually one can find the term *fiducia* in the *Romans Commentary* almost by opening to any page at random. Cf. in the *Apology* also: "We are not talking about a knowledge of history, however, but about *trust* in God's promise and his mercy" (Article 4, para. 337, p. 159).

310. In the 1559 *Loci,* for example, cf. 349, 13; 360, 34 f.; 361, 2 f.; 362, 5 f.; 363, 5 f.; 364, 18 f.; 370, 11 f.; 371, 22 f.; 393, 2; 384, 5 f.; 388, 13 f.; 390, 32 f.; 415, 31 f.; 417, 7 f.; 426, 10 f.

311. *Apology,* Article 4, para. 71, p. 116.

312. *Ibid.,* para. 72, p. 117.

313. 1535 *Loci,* 443.

314. *Apology,* Article 4, para. 50, p. 114. Cf. *ibid.,* para. 324, p. 157.

315. StA V, 65, 13 f. Cf. *ibid.,* 41, 13 f.

316. *Ibid.,* 133, 36-134, 4. Cf. *Apology,* Article 4, para. 76, p. 117.

317. *Apology,* Article 4, para. 158, p. 129.

318. *Ibid.,* para. 182, p. 132. Even the statement just quoted above continues by exchanging reconciliation with forgiveness as justification: ". . . for Christ's sake. Therefore it is clear that we are justified by

faith, for it is sure that we receive the forgiveness of sins by faith alone" (para. 158, p. 129).

Cf. *ibid.*, para. 186, p. 132: ". . . we receive the forgiveness of sins and reconciliation. . . ."

Cf. *ibid.*, Article 15, para. 5, p. 215, and the *Romans Com.* 30, 24; 31, 8.

319. *Romans Com.*, 134, 1 f. Cf. *ibid.*, 134, 9 f.; 99, 9 f., 16 f.

320. *Ibid.*, 135, 3 f.

321. *Apology*, Article 4, para. 293, p. 152.

322. *Ibid.*, para. 307, p. 154.

323. *Ibid.*, para. 305, p. 154. This completes the development beginning with the 1519 Baccalaureate Thesis No. 10 and the statement from the 1523 John Commentary (cf. above, Ch. I, fn. 142 and pp. 45 f.)

324. He speaks also of *merita aliena* ("another's merits") *Romans Com.*, 190, 25; 287, 32, and *propter aliud nos* ("on account of something outside of us"), 215, 34.

325. For example: "For 'grace' means the forgiveness of sins, reconciliation, or the imputation of righteousness. . . ." *Romans Com.* 104, 7 f.

326. *Ibid.*, 184, 21—185, 8.

327. *Formula of Concord*, Article 3, Aff. Thesis No. 1, p. 473.

328. *Ibid.*, para. 252, p. 143, Cf. *ibid.*, para. 305, p. 154: "In this passage 'justify' is used in a forensic way to mean 'to absolve a guilty man and pronounce him righteous'. . . ."

It should be mentioned that Melanchthon did not coin the exact term "forensic justification."

329. Cf. 1532 *Romans Commentary*, 39, 10 f.; 1535 *Loci*, 421. Melanchthon mentions this example quite often in his later works.

330. Melanchthon often equates one or the other, as "pronounced righteous, that is, accepted as righteous" (1535 *Loci*, 415, 439) or "pronounced righteous, that is, forgiven." On successive pages of the 1535 Loci he translates Genesis 15:6 (Abraham believed in God, and it was reckoned to him for righteousness") with *reputare* and *pronuntiare*. *Ibid.*, 417, 418.

331. Though we remind ourselves that Melanchthon found the term *iustitia aliena* in the early writings of Luther. Cf. above, Ch. I, fn. 122.

332. *Apology. Ibid.*, Article 4, para. 72 & 78, p. 117. Cf. *ibid.*, para. 117, p. 123; CR 27, 466, 468.

333. Fortunately Prof. Hans Engelland has summarized the arguments and literature for us, in *Melanchthon, Glauben und Handeln* (Munich: Chr. Kaiser Verlag, 1931), p. 541, fn. 18.

334. Indeed, Prof. Otto Ritschl titled his study of the question "The Double Concept of Justification" ("Der doppelte Rechtfertigungsbegriff in der Apologie," *Zeitschrift für Theologie und Kirche*, 1910, pp. 292 f.

335. *Apology*, para. 313, p. 155. "For two things are attributed to faith, namely justification and vivification. By faith we are pronounced

righteous, and by faith we are made alive (vivificamur)." *Romans Com.*, 66, 12 f.

336. CR XXVII, 470.

337. *Apology*, para. 161, p. 129.

338. *Ibid.*, Article 12, para. 131, p. 202.
    Prof. Edmund Schlink explains it this way: "To be reborn is the renewal effected through the Holy Spirit of the old, dead man to life in Jesus Christ. . . . Regeneration means that works are now possible for a man which were previously impossible." *Theologie der Lutherischen Bekenntnisschriften.* Munchen: Chr. Kaiser Verlag, 1948.

339. Prof. Hans Engelland argues that Melanchthon protected the unity of justification and sanctification because for Philip "all the benefits of the Gospel are included in the idea of the forgiveness of sin." Forgiveness in Christ is the source of both. (Introduction to the 1555 *Loci, op. cit.*, p. xl.)

340. "Sometimes, as in the Apology, the words *regeneratio* (rebirth) and *vivificatio* (making alive) are used in place of justification, and then they mean the same thing, even though otherwise these terms refer to the renovation of man and distinguish it from justification by faith." *Epitome*, para. 8, p. 474.
    In the *Solid Declaration,* Melanchthon's statement "Justification is regeneration" is expressly given a "limited sense," limited to the forgiveness of sins and adoption as God's children, and not including "the subsequent renewal which the Holy Spirit works. . . ." *Sol. Decl.* para. 19, p. 542. To be sure, justification had to be distinguished from subsequent good works, but the effect of this formulation and precaution in the *Formula of Concord* on the development of Lutheran doctrine was to separate justification from renewal too sharply. Though he had opened the door for this development, Melanchthon had not intended it, and Luther assuredly would not have welcomed it.

341. 1535 *Loci*, 421. Cf. *ibid.*, 377, 415, 428, 455, 456. Or he writes on occasion that Christ forgives sins and gives the Spirit. *Ibid.*, 519, 472.

342. *Ibid.*, 458.

343. *Ibid.*

344. *Ibid.* Again, Prof. Engelland asserts that "Melanchthon maintains this unity of forgiveness and sanctification in the mission of Christ." (Introduction to the 1555 *Loci, op. cit.*, p. xxxix.)

345. *Ibid.*, 474.

346. "Our churches also teach that this faith is bound to bring forth good fruits and that it is necessary to do the good works commanded by God. We must do so because it is God's will and not because we rely on such works to merit justification before God. . . ."

347. *Apology*, Article 4, para. 122 f., p. 124 f.

348. *Ibid.*, para. 136, p. 126.

349. Cf. 1535 *Loci*, 405 f.

350. *Apology*, Article 4, para. 130, p. 126; para. 174, p. 131; para. 181, p. 132; para. 252, p. 143; para. 269, p. 147; para. 355, p. 161; para. 362, p. 163, para. 368, p. 163. (These last three passages also deal with the question of rewards for good works. Melanchthon says there will be rewards, but does not go deeply into the issue.)

351. *Romans Com.* 134, 35 f.; 150, 10 f.

352. *1535 Loci*, 432. "I say this clearly and plainly: Our obedience is the righteousness of a good conscience or of works, which God commands and which must follow reconciliation." *Ibid.*, 429. Cf. *ibid.*, 431; *Apology*, Article 4, para. 160, p. 129; *Romans Com.*, 215, 24; 216, 6.

353. *Ibid.*, 49, 30 f.

354. *iustitia fidei, iustitia operum utraque.*

355. *1535 Loci*, 439.

356. *1535 Loci*, 430. Cf. *Romans Com.*, 50, 1 f. 266, 29 f.: ". . . he who has Christ or believes in Christ is righteous, and what the law commands he has by imputation, that is, he is reputed righteous even though he has not satisfied the law. Some explain this from the effect, understanding Romans 10:4 ("Christ is the end of the law") to mean that Christ gives us the Holy Spirit for the fulfilling of the law. This interpretation, though it is true, is nonetheless untimely, since we are not reputed righteous because we do the law, but in faith on account of Christ."

This clear predominance of the righteousness of faith over that of works, marks of both Luther and Melanchthon, becomes then a cornerstone of 17th century Lutheran doctrine.

357. *Apology*, Article 4, para. 179, p. 131. Cf. *Romans Com.*, 153, 20. The words usually used are *etiam, etiansi,* and *tametsi,* and they occur with many variations: ". . . even though sinful, unworthy, impure. . . . ," etc. *Apology*, Article 4, para. 270, p. 147; *Romans Com.*, 31, 3; 71, 1, 12, 17; 127, 1; 134, 9; 208, 3; etc.

". . . even though we do not satisfy the law." *Apology*, Article 4, para. 18, p. 109; para. 179, p. 131; para. 270, p. 147; *Romans Com.*, 35, 14; 210, 16; 231, 16; 266, 31.

". . . even though our nature is full of vice." *Romans Com.* 47, 18.

358. *Apology*, Article 4, para. 160, p. 129.

359. *Ibid.*

360. *1535 Loci*, 437.

Chapter IV. CONTROVERSIALIST

361. Cf. Robert Stupperich's fine summary, "The War, Interim and the Religious Peace," in *Melanchthon*, pp. 122 f., and Clyde Manschreck's introduction to the 1555 *Loci, op. cit.*, pp. xvii, xviii.

362. *Epitome*, Article 10, para. 4, p. 493.

363. *Ibid.*, para. 1, p. 492.

364. *Epitome, ibid.*, para. 7, p. 493; *Sol. Decl., ibid.*, para. 31, p. 616.

"Here we are dealing primarily with the chief article of our Christian faith, so that, as the apostle testifies, the truth of the Gospel might be preserved (Gal. 2:5)." *Sol Decl.*, para. 14, p. 613.

Both the *Epitome* and the *Sol. Decl.* quote Irenaeus: "Disagreement in fasting should not destroy agreement in faith." *Epitome*, para. 7, p. 494; *Sol. Decl.*, para. 31, p. 616.

365. Melanchthon, we remember, wrote in the *Confession*, "It is necessary to do the good works commanded by God" (Article 6). He had also said occasionally, "Good works are necessary," but had long since dropped that, because it was too misleading.

366. 1535 *Loci*, 376.

367. 1559 *Loci*, 243, 14 f.

368. CR XXIII, 15.

369. CR XXIII, 46.

370. *Ibid.*

371. CR IX, 100 f.

372. The *Formula* rejected, for example, the party who said that human nature has "the faculty, aptitude, skill, or ability to *initiate and effect* something in spiritual matters . . ." (*Sol. Decl.*, Article 1, para. 23, p. 512). Melanchthon had certainly stated clearly enough that men couldn't "initiate" anything in "spiritual matters." The *Formula* also said that "the chief issue is solely and alone what unregenerated man's intellect and will can do in his conversion and regeneration, by those powers of his own that have remained after the Fall" (*Ibid.*, Article 2, para. 2, p. 520). Again, Melanchthon had been explicit in denying man any ability of man's intellect and will in his initial conversion. The following paragraph (Para. 3), describing the "Philippists" does not reflect Philip's own teachings.

373. Cf. CR VII, 780, 884, 885. Ubiquity for Melanchthon refers always to the person of Christ: "We believe that these words, 'This is my body,' should be understood as they sound: Christ is truthful and omnipotent, willing and able to be present everywhere, whenever he promises to be by his word." CR IX, 99.

374. CR IX, 99.

375. CR VIII, 910.

376. Cf. for example the letters to Duke John Albert and the city of Wesel cited above.

377. CR VII, 887.

378. *Ibid.* Cf. CR IX, 410.

379. CR VIII, 908. Cf. CR IX, 99, 277, 278, 371, 962.

380. CR VIII, 941, IX, 99, 276, 333, 371, 1040.

381. CR VII, 887.

382. CR IX, 276.

In rejecting this "idolatrous" view of the Supper, there is no indication that Philip was repudiating Luther's emphasis on Christ's physical

presence, as Prof. Manschreck would lead us to believe (Preface to
the 1555 *Loci, op. cit.,* p. xvii). Melanchthon was clearly taking aim
at the Roman view.

383. CR IX, 1040.

384. CR IX, 277, 962. This sort of thinking becomes ridiculous, Melanchthon writes, when one must wonder if a mouse who eats consecrated
bread after the Eucharist is consuming the body of Christ. CR VII,
877.

385. CR IX, 277. Or often Melanchthon will use the ablative case, which
is translated "in," "through," "by means of," etc.: "The Lord's Supper
is that eating, that is reception, in which according to Christ's own
words his body and blood are given to those partaking. Christ is
present by means of the visible elements, bread and wine" (. . . *qui
adest rebus visibilibus, pani et vino),* CR IX, 1040. Whoever feels that
Melanchthon is more "Calvinist" than "Lutheran" on the basis of his
change from "in and under" to "with" should take special note of this
use of the ablative. Not only does the above quote show that Christ's
presence as a person includes his physical nature (i.e., body and
blood), but this presence is "by means of" the elements, not some
sort of spiritual accompaniment.

386. *Formula of Concord, Sol. Decl.,* Article 7, para. 33, p. 575. The
Epitome stresses "with," *ibid.,* para. 6, 15, pp. 482. f.

387. "In this document we have intended to set forth primarily our confession and explanation concerning the true presence of the body and
blood of Christ against the Sacramentarians. . . ." *Sol. Decl.,* Art 7,
para. 111, p. 589. Cf. *ibid.,* para. 2-5. pp. 569 f., for a summary of the
"Sacramentarian" position, describing the opponents of the Lutherans.

388. *Ibid.,* para. 108-110, pp. 588 f.

389. Karl Holl, the pioneering Luther scholar, caused much excitement by
claiming that Luther's concept of justification was a righteousness
which God worked within us, an idea which led him to be sympathetic
to Osiander. This resulted in a book defending Osiander by one of
Holl's most gifted followers, Emanuel Hirsch. *Theologie des Andreas
Osiander* (Göttingen, 1919).

390. Osiander calls this *iustitia essentialis Christi,* the "essential righteousness of Christ," or better, "the righteousness of Christ's essence or
being."